Gifts for Your Soul

SIMPLE HEALING TECHNIQUES
FOR EVERYDAY AND EVERYONE

DOUG BUCKINGHAM

BALBOA.
PRESS

A DIVISION OF HAY HOUSE

Balboa Press books may be ordered through booksellers or by contacting:

Balboa Press
A Division of Hay House
1663 Liberty Drive
Bloomington, IN 47403
www.balboapress.com
1 (877) 407-4847

Because of the dynamic nature of the Internet, any web addresses or
links contained in this book may have changed since publication and
may no longer be valid. The views expressed in this work are solely those
of the author and do not necessarily reflect the views of the publisher,
and the publisher hereby disclaims any responsibility for them.

The author of this book does not dispense medical advice or prescribe the use
of any technique as a form of treatment for physical, emotional, or medical
problems without the advice of a physician, either directly or indirectly. The
intent of the author is only to offer information of a general nature to help
you in your quest for emotional and spiritual well-being. In the event you use
any of the information in this book for yourself, which is your constitutional
right, the author and the publisher assume no responsibility for your actions.

Any people depicted in stock imagery provided by Thinkstock are models,
and such images are being used for illustrative purposes only.
Certain stock imagery © Thinkstock.

Balboa Press books may be ordered through booksellers or by contacting:

ISBN: 978-1-5043-8017-1 (sc)
ISBN: 978-1-5043-8018-8 (hc)
ISBN: 978-1-5043-8060-7 (e)

Library of Congress Control Number: 2017907366

Balboa Press rev. date: 02/27/2018

CONTENTS

Foreword...vii

Preface ix

Introduction..xv

Chapter 1   The Three I's Intention, Imagination & Intuition.1

Chapter 2   Sacred Space and Time......................................9

Chapter 3   Synchronicity..13

Chapter 4   Grounding...17

Chapter 5   Energy Protection 31

Chapter 6   Clearing Your Energy 48

Chapter 7   Putting It All Together.....................................54

Chapter 8   Cutting Cords 58

Chapter 9   Relaxing With the Breath 67

Chapter 10   Meditation..74

Chapter 11   Reflection and Journaling................................80

Chapter 12   Gratitude 86

Chapter 13   Positive Self-Talk 93

Chapter 14   Affirmations 98

Chapter 15   Ho'Oponopono 109

Chapter 16   The Inner Smile.. 115

Chapter 17   Mantra 120

Chapter 18   Intuitive Answers..125

Chapter 19   Clutter Clearing..133

Chapter 20   Love Your Self... 141

Chapter 21   Routine is the Route In................................. 155

Chapter 22 Essential Basics 159

Footnote.. 163
Appendix A 165
The Main Chakras... 165
Appendix B 171
Exercises in this Book... 171
Appendix C... 173
Available Audio Recordings................................. 173
About the Author 175

FOREWORD

Over the past few years, it has been my privilege to work with Doug Buckingham. During this time I have been able to witness his passion for teaching and accompanying people on their personal journey. I have enjoyed seeing the transformation of his clients and students, and have admired him for his practical way of keeping it simple, yet highly effective. Doug is more than just a teacher; he brings a strong intuition to his healings and the capacity to tune into a very strong spiritual connection which is a gift he has developed.

Doug is active and passionate about whatever topic he focuses his intention, as evidenced in his constant search to reach out and accompany people on their personal transformation. He does this by continually structuring new courses, creating applications, making audios, producing webinars and most recently, by writing this highly practical book.

Gifts for Your Soul is clear, concise and complete, and it is a delight to read. This book covers a broad range of simple healing techniques and daily practices. You might use some of these practices on a daily basis, while others, will prove helpful when needed. You can also use this book to enhance your Soul's journey and growth, and you will very soon start noticing the transformation in your daily life. I know I will.

Now that you have this book in your hands, enjoy these **Gifts for Your Soul**.

Carmen Martinez Jover,
Author, Workshops Leader & Infertility Expert

PREFACE

This book contains a collection of simple healing techniques that are easy to carry out on an everyday basis, and in some cases are essential to your ongoing well-being. Some of these techniques may be new to you, whilst others may be familiar, and so may be a welcome reminder for you. All of them are fairly uncomplicated, and all are highly effective. The idea of putting them in one place in a comfortably sized volume is that they are more easily accessible, and so easy to remember, use, and integrate on an everyday basis.

I call this book and those techniques "Gifts for Your Soul", for that is exactly what they are. As energetic beings, or Souls, having a human experience, when we take care of our personality, human self, and energy field, then we also care for our Soul self. These techniques help us to integrate our Soul reality into the human experience more easily, and then they can help us to live our lives from a bigger picture or Soul perspective, that is deeply comforting and infinitely more rewarding than a small time, one life perspective.

I believe that one of the evolutionary tasks for many of you in this lifetime is to learn to take full responsibility for yourself. While this obviously relates to taking responsibility for your finances, relationships, how you feed yourself, and all the other practical tasks of life, it also relates to how you take care of your energetic self, and very importantly managing your thoughts, emotions et al. Often, when a new or renewed enthusiasm for managing your energy takes place in your life, then it means that a lot of the other every day "physical" responsibilities of life become a lot easier to manage too. That learning, or perhaps remembering, that we have the power within us to understand, change and create our own lives, is perhaps one of the most liberating and thrilling concepts available to us all today.

One simple way that you can take responsibility, and also care of yourself, is by ensuring that you have some kind of simple kind of regular practice that enables you to maintain your energetic well-being and thus your mental, physical, and emotional well-being too. In addition to that practice, it also pays dividends to have to hand a series of simple, yet effective techniques that you can use on the occasions when you happen to lose your energetic equilibrium. And all of these possibilities are what this book contains.

In 2018 or whenever you happen to read this book, we live in an age where the health systems of many countries are starting to creak and groan under the pressure that they have been put, and the lack of finances and resources they have been provided with. While that is, in many ways, quite shameful, it is also quite interesting. As a consequence of this, what has been happening is that many more individuals, and many more mental and physical health professionals, are starting to investigate complementary, alternative, or holistic forms of therapy and thus return to what is an age old concept — i.e., that the source of many forms of disease is rooted in our spiritual essence, in our Soul. And perhaps, you are one of those people who is living on what is likely to turn out to be the cutting edge of human evolution, as we start to realise and put fully into practice the reality that we are more than just physical bodies.

I believe that there is an innate ability to self-heal within all of us; as though it is part of our collective DNA. While it is still very much part of the philosophy of many indigenous communities around the world, much of the impulse to self-heal has either been lost or lies more dormant in many parts of the Western World. Here, we have tended to look at dis-ease and imbalance as something that comes from the external world, and have become victims that have to look outside of ourselves to others to fix us.

When we do contract illness or disease, it is important to realise that we have options that are within us as well as outside of us. The innate self-healing ability of the immune system is the most powerful and important healer that we can ever access. What we need to do is to learn how to activate and use that ability within us.

Part of the simple genius of self-healing tools is the fact they also focus on prevention perhaps more than, though certainly as well as, remedy. Scientific research has found that many disorders including heart disease, diabetes, and cancer have been preventable. When we put effort and order into maintaining ourselves, we go some way towards fostering that attitude and state of prevention, which is effectively the ultimate form of self-care. Taking responsibility for generating and maintaining our own well-being is integral for our evolutionary journey as human beings. Evidence for this reality is everywhere. Research studies continually show us that diet, exercise and stress management are some of the most effective tools for maintaining health, and the same applies to personal energy management.

One of the other ideas behind this book is that healing and therapy can be a costly thing, especially for those on a low income. However, not everything about it necessarily needs to be, and that is one reason why this book has been written, which is so that more people can access the simple yet effective healing modalities offered within it. I hope that you can use this concise volume to help you to bring significant changes to your own life. Going to a well-trained practitioner when serious stuff comes up, can, and should, be immensely rewarding for your ongoing well-being, and is usually worth it. However, it is also something that not everyone believes they can afford.

This book provides a few simple, effective tools that are very useful for ongoing maintenance that are on the whole, free. There are some situations where it might be a good idea to go to a class or see a trained professional, and hone some of the skills mentioned here. On the whole, though, the ethos of this book is to keep things simple and manageable in all areas wherever possible.

While this preface may seem to indicate otherwise, another one of the intentions of this book is that it will be concise wherever possible. I am a person who loves the bullet point that tells me everything I need to know rather than the long-winded explanation that sometimes may create confusion rather than clarity. So, everything will be explained concisely and precisely as often as is possible.

Some of the topics that are covered in the various chapters that follow merit a book or two by themselves and the intention here is to highlight these subjects rather than cover them in depth. Perhaps, though, this book will spark your intuition or curiosity to explore the subject of that particular topic more deeply for yourself which is wonderful. There are also practical exercises in many of the chapters in this book to give you opportunities to practice many of the techniques in a simple, effective way.

Finally, you can also access Life Enhancing audio recordings either on my App "Hypnosis for Transformation" — which is available at the App Store and on Android – through my website or Amazon. While these audios are stand-alone products by themselves, they also complement some of the exercises in this book, and you may find them helpful.

Enjoy!

Doug Buckingham

Soul Suggestion

Once you commit to taking responsibility for your own energy, then you can live the difference and feel the benefits.

INTRODUCTION

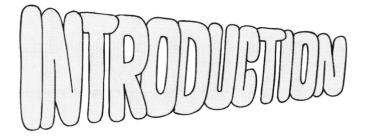

"Enhance Your Energy, and You Will Enhance Your Life"

In an age where we need to put disclaimers in books, I should start off by saying that none of the techniques in this book are substitutes for any medical treatment and if you have a serious medical condition, then you should consult a Doctor or an appropriate specialist.

It also needs to be said that while all of the techniques in this book are magical in nature; they are, alas, not magic wands and if you really want to master these Gifts for Your Soul, then practice does need to be undertaken. I use the word practice quite deliberately, for I have always shied away from the word discipline and I know that others may do likewise. For me, there is an implication in discipline that suggests some kind of rules or restraint that might come from some source outside of ourselves, or some other form of externally imposed values.

Practice, on the other hand, both implies and generates an air of willingness to improve on the part of the individual and nurtures the idea of self-development that this book tries to champion, and I cannot recommend regular practice highly enough for the techniques that follow. The human energy system, the subconscious mind, and the Soul all recognise when you are putting that practice in and respond accordingly and positively.

I once had a client when I lived in the east of London who came for a Reiki session whenever he was totally burnt out. He worked in a high-pressure environment in the main business area of London, and on average he came for a session somewhere between six to eight weeks when he was at that place of burn-out. His usual words after the initial consultation, and before plopping on my healing couch were "Fix me, please!"

After a few episodes of this, I suggested to the client (who had also trained in Reiki) that he might want to be a bit more proactive, rather than reactive, and book himself in for regular sessions so that he could avoid the "burn out." After some reflection, he agreed and booked more regular monthly sessions, and thereafter his energy levels soon blossomed. He slept better, exercised more often, and spent less time at work while accomplishing more. Then he took the proverbial bull by the horns and started coming every fortnight and then his life changed dramatically. Within a couple of months, he got offered an excellent job in his home country, met the partner of his dreams, and had a "happy ever after" life. He emailed after a few months of living back home to confirm he was still having regular "me time" Reiki as well as engaging with his own Reiki self-practice, and that life was still rather sweet.

Make the effort and commitment to yourself, and then the rewards come is the message from that story. That can be a common enough scenario in any circumstance of life, however, it is especially so with energy work. The rewards may not be to the extent related to the story above. However, they will be there in some shape or form if you start to become more conscious of what you need to do for you, and then practice it regularly.

On the subject of what you need to do for you, all of the techniques in this book can work for you and benefit the mind, body, and Soul, however they are complementary techniques in the sense that you do need to be on top of the blindingly obvious first and take care of your basic needs on a physical level. If you are unsure what that may mean, then you may want to have a look at Chapter 22 right away. Otherwise, let's move on to chapter 1.

CHAPTER 1

The Three I's Intention, Imagination & Intuition

Intention

"Intention is one of the most powerful forces there is. What you mean when you do a thing will always determine the outcome. The Law creates the world."

Brenna Yovanoff

Probably the most important thing to remember for all of the techniques that are mentioned in this book is that "Intention is everything." Energy flows where your intention (and attention) goes and having wisdom about how you use your energy in that respect is something everyone can benefit from.

One of the laws that govern our universe is Heisenberg's Uncertainty Principle, which states that we cannot observe something without changing that which we are observing. According to Heisenberg, there is no such thing as an independent observer. Other principles of quantum physics state the observer influences the experiment - i.e., that our consciousness or more specifically <u>our intention</u> influences what happens in our external reality.

Equally, our intention can affect the degree of success with which energy management and healing techniques succeed. The bottom line when working with energy is always try to keep an open mind, and a positive intention towards the technique that you are working with, and also to yourself.

It is important to have an intention for the energy work or healing exercise that you do. When you do, you are likely to find you achieve much more from the process than you expected. Keep in mind that the overriding intention for any session or exercise is that it is for the highest good (of you or another). When you have this intention, then you are working in line with the Soul perspective of the other or of yourself. In these instances, bear in mind that you may not always get what you as the personality wants, however, you are likely to get what you, as the Soul, needs.

Intention, in more everyday language and for the purposes of this book, can be quite simply thought of as a goal or objective for the particular healing exercise(s) that you are practicing.

> **<u>Soul Suggestion</u>**
> *Have a clear intention when*
> *you are working with energy*

Imagination

"Logic will get you from A to B.
Imagination will take you everywhere."

Albert Einstein

Some of the exercises that you will find in this book refer to the imagination or more specifically ask you to imagine something. Many people like to use the term "visualisation." In my opinion, that is a limiting term for the simple reason that not everyone is primarily visual when they tune into their inner senses. I know and have taught, some very talented healers and therapists who are not visual in any shape or form. Some are kinaesthetic (feeling), others are knowing, or knowers, some auditory, and numerous people tune into their intuition by a combination of the above, rather than solely the visual aspect.

Generally speaking, any form of imagination or visualisation exercise is enhanced by the use of as many of the senses as possible, and even the less obvious ones like smell can be a particularly potent resource within the inner senses. I have not always counted myself as an especially visual person, and I remember that was the case, the first time I experienced a full-length past life regression. As I drifted into a hypnotic trance, I became aware of a particularly pungent smell in my inner world. By tuning into that smell, I knew exactly where I was and more importantly, I knew what the story was. (About 200 years ago in Napoleon's Army, surrounded by dead or dying soldiers on a battlefield, for the curious amongst you.)

When you tune into a regression, meditation experience, shamanic journey, or any process for your inner world, your intention is present at the start of the session. That evokes your imagination (the inner senses and the language of the Soul) to take you into the memories and feelings of that experience within your inner world. You can then allow yourself to be guided in whatever way those inner senses communicate to you so that you flow easily and naturally within your experience.

Equally, when you are visualising or imagining your roots going down into the centre of the Earth (as in the grounding or other exercises that follow), then your imagination works hand in hand with your intention to assist those roots, so they have the maximum "chance" of helping you to ground your energy. Energy follows intention. It is a law of the Universe, Quantum Physics, and it just IS.

Another example of your imagination working wonderfully well is when you daydream, reflect, or muse about the future. At the heart of your consciousness, you are a creative being, and when you project your energy into the near or distant future, then you are starting to create a possible situation which may well come to fruition if you give it enough energy (imagination and intention in this case) on a regular basis.

A negative example of this is 'worry'. When you worry about something, then you project that energy, which in this case is fear of what might happen, into your future. In doing this, you may well negatively impact your own nervous system, and especially so if you are a consistent worrier. Furthermore, you may also increase the chances of actually creating the situation you are worrying about, which is what you do not want of course.

A positive example of this is something called "future creation" which I use a lot in hypnosis. Here, the client imagines future scenarios based on their goal for therapy while they are in trance. For example, a client whose intention is to become a more confident public speaker might have an actual speaking engagement to perform a month or so in the future. In a comfortable state of relaxation, which is what hypnosis is, they imagine that future scenario with whatever senses work best for them. Very importantly, they also connect with the emotions of that future image of themselves and feel that "future" emotion flowing through them now. Future creation is an extremely powerful and useful process, especially when you are working with hypnosis and doing it repetitively, and even more especially when you connect with the positive emotions that are associated with achieving your objective.

One of the reasons why this technique works so well is that the subconscious mind does not differentiate between what we refer to as reality and the imagined reality. Consequently, it starts to generate positive energy, thoughts, and feelings based on that future possibility, and that then heightens the possibility of that future becoming a reality.

The concept that your thoughts and positive emotions are able to significantly change your reality is something that a lot of scientists starting to experiment in the spiritual arena are catching onto in a big way at the moment, and this knowledge is, fortunately, becoming much more mainstream. Remember, when you harness the potential of your imagination in a positive way, then it can bring highly beneficial experiences into your reality.

> **Soul Suggestion**
> *Imagination is the language of the Soul. Use it positively and wisely to help you to change your reality now!*

Intuition

"Your time is limited, so don't waste it living someone else's life. Don't be trapped by dogma which is living with the results of other people's thinking. Don't let the noise of others' opinions drown out your own inner voice. And most important, have the courage to follow your heart and intuition."

Steve Jobs

Perhaps the most important thing to remember about intuition is that everyone is born intuitive. Some people might seem naturally more intuitive than others. The truth is, though, that intuition is a natural ability that we all have. Whether you choose to call that intuition, instinct, gut feeling or something else does not really matter, as it all part of the same thing.

Many people forget about their intuitive abilities, some have it conditioned out of them by other people's or society's beliefs systems and some even deliberately let it go, in case it gets them into "trouble." Whatever the circumstances though, it never disappears completely. You could think of your intuition like a muscle, and the more you acknowledge that you have it and the more you use it, then the stronger and more reliable it becomes. If, however, you do not use it very often, then it is likely to be weaker and might well be in need of a little work-out. Often those people that are highly intuitive are generally those that have practiced and learnt to trust their intuition as a result of that practice.

One of the things that many people do in the spiritual world is go to others for guidance or readings. If you are doing that to help validate or work with your own intuitions, then that is wonderful, as there are many great readers out there who can complement what you are thinking, or feeling, or perhaps slightly unsure about. Then again, if you are doing that instead of trying to listen to your intuition, then think about the message you are sending to yourself - which is essentially "I do not trust myself enough" or "I am not intuitive (good?) enough" or something similar. There are, of course, times when you need a second opinion, or some external guidance, to help you along the journey in life, and it is important to recognise that and then reach out for help. However, I suggest that you do that from a point of empowerment and avoid letting it be at the expense of your own sense of self-worth.

Intuition is for you — as it is short for "inner-tuition" — so that is you teaching yourself. Trusting your own intuition is of paramount importance, and it tends to be more of a process than an event with most people. It can take time to trust that inner voice, especially when trusting it often involves going against what may present itself as logic.

I am fortunate to have been blessed with a strong inner knowing in this life. I have not always actively listened to it though, and so re-learning my intuition when I began a more overtly spiritual journey in my life became a passion for me. I remember one particular morning I got up to go to work, which was over an hour's journey by public transport to the other side of London. My normal journey was by River Boat, followed by underground and it was straight-forward and got me to work with ten minutes to spare when everything flowed. That morning my intuitive knowing said 'catch the bus, then the underground, change trains and go via the centre of London.'

The route my intuitive voice was suggesting actually made no logical sense as the journey would take considerably longer this way. However, at the time I was on a mission to listen to my intuition, and so that is what I did. In the centre of London, I found my way to a spiritual bookshop which was just opening for the day. There I found a leaflet advertising a holistic therapy room which I ended up renting for the next year and a half. Had I followed my logic, it is unlikely that would have happened.

Curiously, I made it to work still with five minutes to spare, even by the much longer route. I have countless examples of similar events and anecdotes in my own life, and I am sure you probably have one or two too. When you can start to remember these in a positive light, and when you learn and yearn to trust yourself even more, then you will. Trust in your intuition is a wonderful asset to have in any walk of life, and you can grow it with simple everyday activities if you choose to. You can read more about that in Chapter 18.

Intention, Imagination & Intuition

Working with the three I's needs to become second-nature to you when you are developing yourself in the energy world. In the same way that mirror-signal-manoeuvre becomes an instinctive and automatically remembered process when you been driving a car for a while, then positively using your intention, listening to your imagination, and trusting your intention are key skills along your energetic management and spiritual development road.

> **Soul Suggestion**
> *Magical things happen when you align your intention, your imagination and your intuition.*

CHAPTER 2

Sacred Space and Time

"Sacred space is another way of saying with intention"

S Kelley Harrell

Sacred Space

Having a sacred or special place for you in which to practice some of the ideas and techniques in this book is very valuable. That does not necessarily mean that you must have a dedicated room, though if you do, that is perfect. Creating a space or spot in your living area where you come to get in touch with yourself and your Soul has meaning, for it sends a message to all parts of you that are making the effort. And making that effort is in some ways more important than the actual result.

If you have a flat or house, you might like to dedicate a room or section of it to your practice. If you have only have one room in which you live or limited space, then you might choose to dedicate a corner or small area of it to be a sacred space for you. If possible, try and be consistent in the actual space that you use, i.e. avoid changing rooms or corners every couple of days. Strange as it might sound, the more you actually use that same space for carrying out your energy management practice, then the more that space will respond to you.

Objects which you value and consider sacred can be placed in this area. The choice is obviously yours, though perhaps a candle, incense, totem of some description, pictures, crystals, or anything else which you consider meaningful will help to create the ideal energy in this space for you. Some people like to have representations of the four elements in their space: for example - air=incense, candle=fire, crystal=earth, and a glass of water or whatever takes your fancy for the water element. This is a lovely way to invoke the positive energy of the natural world into your sacred space, and it can be tremendously helpful for your overall well-being to honour the elements in this way. If you would like to go a step further, then you might like to place air pointing east in your space, fire to the south, water to the west and earth to the north, and honour the four directions as well as the four elements. When creating your sacred space remember that the quality or amount of space that you have to practice in and the quality of the objects that you put into it are both secondary to the intention that you put into your space.

Please note that if your space is part of an area that you have to share with others, then it is worth speaking to those whom you share it with, and asking them to acknowledge and respect what it means for you. If that is something that is genuinely unachievable, then start thinking about looking for a different space, where you can maintain your own energetic integrity more comfortably and easily.

Sacred Time

Just as valuable as sacred space is sacred time. Reflect for a moment on what a wonderful message you are sending to yourself if you make the decision to spend five or even fifteen quality minutes each morning practicing some simple, yet highly beneficial techniques that enhance your energy, and thus brighten up your day and your prospects for that day and each day that follows it.

When you can make regular time for yourself each day, then you are reinforcing a powerful and positive message to yourself. You might be able to do this as soon as you get out of bed, though if not, any time is perfectly good. The amount of time is of secondary importance to the value and intention that you put into what time you actually have available to you. If you only have five minutes in the morning because of important commitments, then use that time wisely and with a good, clear focus and intention.

If though, you only have five minutes because you cannot be bothered to get out of bed each day, then you probably are not approaching your time with yourself with the best of intentions.

By the way, it is entirely possible to use some of the suggestions in this book while lying comfortably in bed. It is perhaps not the perfect spot, though nonetheless they still work wherever you are with a good intention behind them.

Remember when making your time sacred, that intention is key. When you do things by rote, or out of some form of half-hearted obligation, then that also reflects into the intention of whatever it is that you are doing. So, when you are making some of your valuable time available to practice energy techniques, then I suggest that you do them with a good level of enthusiasm and positivity in order to maximise the effect that you might get out of them. Otherwise, why are you bothering?

Although I am a firm believer in reincarnation, I also know that time in this incarnation is finite. Therefore, I am an equally firm believer in devoting your precious spare time to things that you have a genuine faith in, respect for and enjoy and benefit from. For example, I would not spend a substantial period of time writing this book, if a) I did not believe in its ability to make a difference, and b) I did not enjoy doing writing it. So, use your own precious time mindfully, and make it sacred when you do.

Soul Suggestion
Space and time only exist within the context of your human experience, so give them freely and willingly to yourself.

CHAPTER 3

Synchronicity

'Synchronicity holds the promise that if we want to change inside, the patterns of our external life will change as well.'

Jean Shinoda Bolen

Carl Jung is reported to have said that "synchronicity is an ever-present reality for those with the eyes to see." Jung is, in fact, credited with coining the term synchronicity and developed several definitions of it. One of the most succinct of those says that events are "meaningful coincidences" if they occur with no causal relationship yet seem to be meaningfully related. Synchronicity is the experience of two or more events that are apparently causally unrelated or unlikely to occur together by chance, actually occurring together in a meaningful manner.

Synchronicities present themselves more obviously in life when you start to engage with your Soul Journey, whereupon what is present in the subconscious or Soul mind starts to make itself more manifest into your conscious reality. When you venture deep enough into the subconscious, then these correlations between the conscious and the subconscious become how life is, rather than an occasional surprise, as the walls between your inner world and the outer reality you create begin to dissolve. Synchronicities are one way that the Soul shows you that you are "on track."

The story that Jung told of a client in his practice is a perfect example of how observing synchronicities can be helpful to anyone's process. The story goes that he had a young, female patient who was extremely well educated and was what he called "psychologically inaccessible," due to her excellent ability to rationalise everything in her life. She had been in therapy for a while and was particularly resistant to the concept of relating her dreams to Jung. During one session Jung had finally managed to persuade her about the importance of her dream for the psychoanalytical process. She then told him about an impressive dream that she had the night before, wherein the dream someone had given her a golden scarab which was a costly piece of jewelry. While she was still telling Jung this dream, he heard something behind him gently tapping on the window. When he turned round, he saw that it was a fairly large flying insect knocking against the window-pane from outside trying to get into the room. Upon opening the window, he caught the insect as it flew in, and discovered that it was a scarabaeid beetle, whose gold-green colour nearly resembles that of a golden scarab. He promptly handed the beetle to the client saying, "Here is your scarab." This deflated her rationalism, broke her intellectual resistance, and therapist and client were able to continue with therapy with excellent results.

Likewise, when you find your own inner world manifesting into external reality, then it is time to pay attention. The synchronicity may be a sign you are reading the 'right' book, meeting the 'right' person, etc. Bear in mind though, that a synchronicity does not necessarily mean that everything will turn out perfectly, for synchronicity is merely a vindication that you are on the next step of your Soul Path, and what our Soul has in store for us is not always what our personality wants. Nevertheless, we always get what the Soul needs.

More scientifically minded people may dismiss potential synchronicities as apophenia, which is defined as seeing false patterns in random or meaningless data. It is very easy to dismiss anything if you really want to, and equally, it is quite simple to build too much meaning into something which may not really hold much relevance for you.

Synchronicity is an indicator of potential, and the only way to find out its real relevance for your journey is to approach it with a clear and open mind, and then test it out in real life. One of the ways to work with synchronicities and develop a greater understanding of their potential for you is to approach them in the same way that works well with dreams. Start making notes about them, however trivial the synchronicities might appear to be. The recognition alone of the synchronicity heightens that connection between the Soul and the personality self. Once that connection strengthens, it becomes easier to get an authentic knowing for the importance of the synchronicity. At that point, you will either start to notice more of them, or more will start happening. Chicken or egg?

As you keep track of synchronicities happening in your life, you can also develop a greater feeling for them and their significance to you. You may well become more aware of patterns that surround them, and might even start to develop a greater understanding of what is being triggered in your subconscious that creates these meaningful happenings. Remember that awareness and ownership of your part in reality creation are vital steps to manage your own energy and as a result, your life.

> ## Soul Suggestion
> *Your Soul knows the "Plan" and is trying to help you to remember it. So be watchful and act upon synchronicities.*

CHAPTER 4

Grounding

"There is deep wisdom within our very flesh, if we can only come to our senses and feel it.

Elizabeth A. Behnke

Grounding yourself is a way of being fully in your body, and it is an essential part of energy management. Some people are more prone than others to being in their heads, not being firmly rooted in them, or even leaving their bodies altogether. Anybody who does energy work needs to ground their energies on a regular basis, and it is a beneficial practice for absolutely everyone as we are all energetic beings at our core. This is becoming more important every day with stronger and more powerful energies being present on the planet.

Grounding helps you to reconnect your energy body with the energy of the Earth so that you can carry the vitality that comes from the Earth more easily. If you think about it, the energy of the Earth is a fundamental part of what sustains and nurtures all life on this planet, and that includes you. So, you actually need to have a conscious connection as well as an unconscious connection with it, and that connection is grounding.

Just like electrical plugs need a grounding prong so that they do not build up excess "charge" (read stress for humans) or even short-circuit, your energy field also needs to ground. While doing so, it also helps to balance and strengthen the chakras and the aura, all of which are electromagnetic in nature, and all of which connect directly into your physical and emotional energy, and thus your entire life.

Your immune system, which is connected to the chakras, also functions optimally when your body has an adequate supply of electrons, which are obtained by contact with the Earth. This is another reason grounding can also be a way of coping with stress, as it is essentially calming and helps to induce stillness within you. When you have a balanced, still energy field, it means you are less likely to take on energies that do not belong to you (see next chapter), and both of these factors will contribute to having higher energy levels and being less tired. For those people who find that they are struggling to create the life that they want to live, grounding can often be the first important step in successful energy management; for "Grounding is the foundation on which all else is based."

When people are ungrounded, there is often an associated feeling of light-headedness. The feeling can be similar to having a few drinks, though without the cost and the potential hangover the next day. Even if that does sounds like fun, it is very much short-termist thinking.

There are valid reasons why people are ungrounded. It is a reality that a lot of people on the planet live "from the neck upwards" and are less in touch with their bodies than our ancestors, who were versed in using the physical body in their work, often as a means of getting to work, and within much more of their everyday life in general.

Sometimes people dissociate from their bodies because of a trauma earlier in their life and find it more challenging to be fully present in their body later in life. Most often that is an unconscious protection measure, as it is a very good way to disconnect from painful emotions, physical sensations, and pain in general. There may even be a physical illness which is associated with the inability to ground, and not wanting to feel the physical pain may be a good enough reason not to stay grounded in the body. Some people come to Earth with very high levels of energy, simply do not want to be here on the planet or do not feel that they belong, and that can cause a general feeling of not being connected or grounded. However, we all made a choice on a Soul level to be here, and grounding is an excellent way to make sure we are here and are able to journey through what we came here to do or to be, however challenging that may be.

Without grounding, you can become unstable and literally lose your centre, which could result in lack of physical balance or ongoing problems with dizziness, or feeling confused on a regular basis. Problems with concentration, attention span or being unable to truly listen to others are all symptoms of being ungrounded. For some, the lack of grounding manifests as getting physically lost (losing connection with magnetic core of the Earth) on a regular basis, or problems with punctuality. Long-term lack of grounding can also result in serious damage to both your physical and even your mental health and no-one really wants to go there.

Simple Techniques to Stay Grounded

The good news is that there are many simple ways to keep yourself grounded in daily life and without too much effort. For example:

- Concentration or mindfulness on the breath
- Paying attention to the body - people often do simple tasks such as going to the toilet or doing household chores without any focus on their body or its sensations. These seemingly simple moments are actually opportunities to be conscious of how your physical body is responding, and to have authentic contact with it.
- Walking in a mindful way
- Being in nature
- Eating healthy food
- Walking barefoot on the Earth (see also Earthing at the end of this chapter)

Anything that brings you back into being fully present in your body is basically grounding. Nonetheless, it is also smart to practice grounding exercises. If this is a new concept for you, then it is worthwhile to ensure that you practice them with care and attention when you first start. Then, after a while, it is likely you will be able to either ground more quickly or do it instantly, with the same amount of care and attention or do it almost semi-consciously and yet still effectively.

Grounding Exercises

When you decide to use a grounding exercise, make the intention to start doing it on a regular basis. Grounding on a regular basis means that your energy system gets used to that connection with the earth, and like anything that you do on a regular basis, it becomes part of your subconscious memory. Then, over time, it becomes easier and more automatic each time that you do it.

For any grounding exercise that you do, I recommend that before you start, you say out loud or even silently to yourself the following affirmation:

"I command all parts of my energy to come back to me here now."

Whilst this might sound slightly odd at first, it is actually an entirely logical thing to do. Grounding is about being in the present moment. Most humans naturally invest energy in past events and also in worrying or thinking about the future, so if you start off your grounding by getting all those energetic parts to come back to you, then it makes your grounding more effective.

Exercise 1 - Breath Awareness

One of the easiest ways to ground is to bring your attention to the breath as it enters and leaves your body, and this draws you into focusing on both your breath and your body.

- Sit down in a comfortable position for you, though you can also do this standing up.
- Closing your eyes is optional. However, it is usually best to shut out your external visual sense (by closing the eyes) to optimise the inner senses.
- Take 10 breaths in and out and pay attention as you do.
- As you start to feel the connection to your physical self, bring your awareness to the sensations in your body.
- You can be aware of where the breath comes in through the nostrils; how it moves down through the airways; how it fills your lungs; the expansion of your rib-cage or possibly the way your stomach pushes out gently and easily as your breathe comes in.
- Stay focused on your breathing as you become aware of these or any other sensations in your body.
- Take your attention from your nostrils where your breath comes in, and move it down your body as though you are following the breath all the way down and then keep following the breath as it goes out of your body.
- While you do this, stay present in your body and avoid drifting off, and feel the various sensations in different parts of your body.
- When you have taken 10 breathes in and out, then feel your feet flat on the floor and your bottom on the chair (if sitting) and see how you feel.

This is fundamentally a simple mindfulness exercise.

Hopefully, after doing this exercise, you will feel more aware of your connection to yourself, more alive and more aware of the sensations in your body.

Exercise 2 – Growing Energetic Roots

- Sit down in a comfortable position for you, though you can also do this standing up. Make sure your feet are flat on the floor.

- Closing your eyes is optional, especially if you are standing or in public. It is usually best to close off the external visual sense (by closing the eyes) to optimise the inner senses.

- Take a couple of breathes in and out, and focus on these breathes are they come in and go out. Make them conscious breathes.

- Then take your attention down to your feet. Get a real sense of the connection of your feet with the floor or the surface beneath you. Put all of your attention on your feet and that connection.

- Then use your imagination and your intention, and imagine that you are growing roots out of the soles of your feet, just like those of a tree, though energetic in this case rather than physical.

- Imagine and intend that you can grow these roots down through the floor that you are present upon, down through the rest of the building, and down through all the layers of the Earth beneath that building and right down into the magnetic core of the Earth, or however you sense the centre of the planet.

- That is all you need to do - imagine growing these energetic roots right out of the soles of your feet and going all the way down into the Earth.

- If you find your roots do not go that far down, then you can imagine attaching a weighted object, perhaps like a ship's anchor or some other heavy object to your roots, to enable you to extend them deeper into the Earth.

- You can be aware of this, perhaps by seeing these roots go down into the energy of the Earth, feeling them go down, knowing that they are going down or getting a sense of them going down in some other way that is meaningful for you.

- As you send the roots down you may also sense the energy within the Earth beneath you. Remember you may see it, feel it, know it, or simply be open to the possibility of energy within the Earth.

- Then, feeling connected or anchored in some way to the centre of the Earth, start to breathe the energy of the Earth up through the roots. Remember that this is energy that helps to sustain and nurture all life on the planet, and that includes you.

- Get a sense of being able to breathe that energy in through the soles of your feet, up through your legs, and up into your spine and up through your body.

- If you have an awareness of the chakra system, then as you breathe, bring the energy through the chakra centres. If not, then imagine breathing the energy up your spine. Again you may see, feel, know, or imagine this happening in any way you like.

- Spend a couple of minutes consciously breathing that energy in, up through the roots from your feet, up through your body and feel the effect that it may have on your body. You may have a sense of expansion, there may be tingling in your body, or you may be aware of sensations that you have been previously unaware of, both in and around your body.

- Be aware of this process as you breathe grounding energy from the centre of the Earth up through your roots and into your body. Be fully present in your body as you do this.
- When you have a good sense of the different feelings in your body, then you are grounded. Feel your feet on the floor, and your bottom on the chair. Then open your eyes and get on with your day.

It may take you a few minutes the first couple of times you do this exercise. However, with a little practice and continued awareness, then you should be able to do it in thirty seconds or so with focused attention.

Exercise 3 – Grounding from the Root or Base Chakra

Even with little or no awareness of the chakra system, this is a simple exercise to do. The root or base chakra is an energetic centre located at the bottom of your spine, in the perineum area between your anus and your genitalia.

- Sit down in a comfortable position for you, though you can also do this standing up.
- Closing your eyes is optional, especially if you are standing or in public.
- Take a couple of breaths in and out, and be aware of your breath.
- Focus your attention on your spine and get a sense of your spine from the bottom to the top of it. As you do, imagine it as a column of light, a silver cord or perhaps simply as energy.

- Focus on the bottom of your spine in that root chakra area around the perineum.

- Imagine, intend and allow yourself to extend the energy of your chakra column (or silver cord) from your root chakra all the way down into the earth.

- In the same way that you can grow roots from the soles of your feet, you are extending the energy from your root chakra all the way down through the floor or surface that you are on, through the different layers of the Earth and all the way down into the core of the Earth.

- If necessary, you can imagine attaching a weighted object to this energy connection that you are making, to extend it deeper into the Earth.

- Use your imagination and your intention with the energy of your spine and allow it to drop deeper and deeper into the Earth. As you do this, you may even feel as you are being pulled downwards or perhaps that your spine is somehow being extended.

- You are now grounded, and your body is likely to be heavier and more relaxed, especially the legs or your feet.

- With that relaxed feeling in place, imagine the energy of the Earth flowing up into your base chakra. In the same way that the roots from your feet brought energy up, you can also bring energy up into your base chakra.

- Now feel that connection to the Earth permanent and stable

- When you feel comfortable with this, feel your feet on the floor, your bottom on the chair, open your eyes and come back into your space.

Exercise 4 - Combining the Roots & the Base Chakra - Recommended

Once you have practiced exercises 2&3, moving on to this exercise is simply combining what you already know from the previous exercises to make your grounding even more effective.

- Again you can do this sitting or standing up. Being comfortable is the key.
- Closing your eyes is optimal.
- Take a couple of breathes in and out, and be aware of your breath as it comes in and goes out of the body.
- Now focus on your feet and imagine dropping roots from each of your feet all the way down into the Earth.
- At the same time extend the energy of your spine from your base chakra down into the centre of the earth. So you are establishing three connections (two from the feet, and one from the base of the spine) at the same time.
- Allow them all to drop deeper and deeper, and you may even feel as though both of your legs and your spine are pulling downwards in some way.
- Take a few moments or even minutes and breathe the grounding, nurturing energy of the earth up through your roots into both of your feet and into your base chakra.
- Your legs may start to feel heavy, and your feet may even feel as if they are stuck to the floor. If you are sitting down, your bottom may feel heavy and perhaps even stuck to the chair.
- This is all normal and means you are now grounding very well.
- Then when you feel that you are grounded, feel your feet on the floor, your bottom on the chair and open your eyes.

What you will have experienced is that while these exercises may take some time to read through and practice, grounding is actually quite simple. Once you have done it a few times, you should be able to ground in much less time than it took you to read the exercises.

A combination of roots from the feet and grounding from the base chakra area is ideal (i.e., the last exercise) however you may find one easier to do than the other, in which case focus on your stronger area to get you grounded at first. Avoid neglecting whichever area is weak though, as it is useful to develop both areas, so keep on practicing both ways until each area is strong.

Grounding is actually very simple and quick to do; you can do it in the shower, or at any time of day you would like to. What you may notice as you practice grounding when you go about your daily life, is that you will become more aware of the times when you become ungrounded. Perhaps certain situations, maybe certain places or even people may spark that feeling of being ungrounded within you. And that is really useful to become aware of, and then do something about. What you have already seen from the grounding exercises is that they are theoretically simple to do so that you can actually do them effectively in 30 seconds or so, and re-ground yourself when you become aware of situations where you lose your grounding. If you find yourself in situations where you become a little more light-headed, confused or some other indication that you have become ungrounded, then you have a simple and effective tool to remedy that quickly.

There are plenty of other ways to ground as well. Some forms of yoga are excellent for grounding because it teaches you about the breath and also to be really alive in your body. Physical exercise is very good when you are focused and not plugged into an iPod or the TV

Contact in nature is excellent, and simply being in the garden or the park helps. Gardening, in particular, is very useful as that is an instant Earth connection.

Resting can also be useful. Often people feel ungrounded because they are doing so much in their daily lives that they do not stay still for long and thus scatter their energy. Sitting and doing nothing, and calling your energy back to you for five or ten minutes can work wonders for your grounding, as well as your general well-being.

Eating is another good short-term grounding technique. Root vegetables are fabulously helpful, and protein is great for the root chakra.

Some people also like to use crystals to enhance their ability to ground. Black tourmaline, pyrite, hematite, galena, smoky quartz are all particularly good for grounding. Keeping them in your pocket works well or somewhere else in your energy field. However, remember that a crystal merely helps you with your ability to make the grounding connection, rather than doing the job for you.

> ### Soul Suggestion
> *Practice grounding at least a couple of times a day, and be conscious about the process. This helps to re-train your energy field so you can experience the benefits of grounding.*

<u>Earthing</u>

As a footnote to grounding, it is also well worth mentioning earthing. This emerging philosophy-cum-science is starting to document how contact with the Earth, or earthing, is very beneficial to your health. This is being in direct contact with the Earth, rather than imagining it, though both are effective. Earthing, in particular, appears to minimize the consequences of exposure to potentially disruptive fields like "electromagnetic pollution" or "dirty electricity."

Research indicates that electrons from the Earth have antioxidant effects that can protect your body from inflammation and its many health consequences. It is known that the Earth maintains a negative electrical potential on its surface, and when you are in direct contact with the ground, perhaps through walking, sitting, or laying down on the earth's surface, then the earth's electrons are conducted to your body, bringing it to the same electrical potential as the earth and allowing you to discharge excess energy.

For the majority of our history, humans have had continuous contact with the Earth, and it is only recently that substances such as concrete, wood, plastics and more have made this contact much less frequent.

Really simple solutions for this are living in direct contact with the Earth or barefoot contact with the Earth when possible. Walking and/or being in nature also work, or if you cannot do either of the above, then grounding exercises work well. Equally, you can now find earthing mats, sheets and other products that do a similar job available for sale on the internet.

CHAPTER 5

Energy Protection

"There are only two kinds of people who can drain your energy: those you love, and those you fear.
In both instances, it is you who let them in. They did not force their way into your aura, or pry their way into your reality experience.

Anton St. Maarten

What is Energy Protection?

The reality is that you are much than just your physical body, and in fact, you have an energy body or an aura all around you. A quick look at something like Kirlian photography on the internet will show you scientific evidence that can reinforce that idea. And, in the same way that you need to take care of your physical body by showering, brushing your teeth, and other daily cleaning habits, it is also healthily beneficial to take care of your energy body.

Your energy body may become congested or sluggish with all of the things you cannot see around you getting caught up in it. In much the same way that dust gathers on physical objects, energy such as old emotions and feelings, thoughts and even other people's energies might get caught up in your energy field, so it is essential practice to clear and cleanse yourself regularly.(Also see energy clearing in the next chapter). As well as curative ideas, though, it is also good sense to have preventative measures in place to ensure your energy field stays as fresh as possible, and this is where energy protection is very useful.

We all have some sort of awareness of unseen energy around us that we can put into context in everyday life; sensing someone else's mood and getting caught up in it, walking into a room where you could cut the atmosphere with a knife, being uncomfortable with certain places or people, etc. The trick is to avoid getting caught up in that energy, or often more pertinently, to avoid allowing that energy to get entangled in your energy field.

Just like you have a skin around you that separates the inside of you from outside elements, you also have a barrier around the outside of your energy field that can help you to maintain the integrity of your aura or energy field, thus preventing any unwanted energy from entering your energy field. The efficiency of that barrier around the outside of your energy field can fluctuate depending on your personal energy levels, your emotional states, and life's circumstances. Therefore, it is very wise to use some form of additional assistance for that barrier which we call energy protection. This helps to maintain the integrity of an individual's aura or electro-magnetic energy field, and so prevent unwanted energy from entering inside it.

Some people like to refer to "negative" energies at this point. Personally, I do not completely resonate with the concept of negative energies as such. Instead, I prefer to use the word inappropriate or the phrase "energies that we do not resonate with," or are unable to master at the moment, or perhaps even simply do not understand. In traditional Chinese medicine, the negative view of any energy does not exist. Instead, the view is that the quality of an energy depends on the context. For example, the energy released by rotting leaves brings fertility to the soil when it is placed upon it, and thus is considered good energy or appropriate. However, when that same energy is in the food that you have recently eaten and enters your stomach, then it is likely to be considered bad, and thus inappropriate. With this logic in mind, there is a place for the rotting leaves; it just needs putting in the appropriate place.

Inappropriate energies are often part of everyday surroundings and can sometimes influence how you choose to feel or respond in certain situations, just as you might feel and act differently depending on the sounds or noises that are present in a space. For example, certain types of music may calm you; others may motivate you and others may simply make you feel uncomfortable. In the same way, certain energies may affect you and your behaviours at certain times. Part of the journey is in recognising this resonance (or non-resonance) within yourself, and learning how to manage your own energy in a positive way when things do not resonate with you. The optimum reality is to keep your energy field strong and protected, and sufficiently so to avoid taking on any inappropriate energies that do not belong to you.

I once had a great anecdote from a Reiki student about the benefits of a positive attitude towards using energy protection:

"There had been rumours of male prowlers in her local area. One dark, foggy winter night as she got out of her car a couple of hundred metres from her home in a badly lit part of the street, she had a sense of someone watching her. She could not see them, so she started to walk away towards her home, and as she did, she heard footsteps behind her. She started to quicken her pace and heard the footsteps quicken behind her too. At this point, she started to feel the natural fear that someone would in that situation and tried desperately to remain calm whilst hearing the footsteps get closer to her.

Then she made a decision and stopped walking. Instead, she focused all of her intention on putting her energy protection in place. The footsteps stopped immediately; presumably at some level the person or prowler had a sense of her strength. Then she carried on walking more slowly than before towards her house. Fortunately, she heard nothing more from anyone behind her."

Whether the energy protection worked, or whether the brave show of calm strength worked does not matter. Probably both of them helped her that night.

Energy Protection Protocol

There are a few important points to remember about energy protection exercises before you get started:

- You draw into your experience things of a similar vibration to the one that you are emanating. This may well be on a deeply subconscious level. Nevertheless, it is still a "signal to the Universe" that you are sending out. Therefore, the intention is especially important in the context of energy protection. What do you want to radiate out into the Universe and attract into your life? The fear of picking up some inappropriate energy or the knowledge that you are "safe, comfortable and protected." The latter is, of course, preferable for everyone. Therefore being positive, confident and knowing that you are fine, rather than being fearful of what might happen if you do not do this or that, is the way forward. Fear is an emotion that lowers your energy vibration, and it can allow inappropriate and unnecessary energies to be attracted into your field, so it is important to avoid radiating that fear out. Instead, think thoughts of comfort and of maintaining the integrity of your energy.

- When applying energy protection techniques, it is important to feel confident in whatever technique that you employ. If you are not confident in your technique, then try another and if you are not confident with that, then go and book a session with a specialist in this area. Confidence or feeling self-assured is really useful for this technique to work well.

- Grounding (in the previous chapter) is of paramount importance. When you are grounded, then some of the protection work is already done.

Energy Protection Exercises

Most energy protection techniques are what are called barrier or prevention methods whereby bubbles, pyramids, cloaks, shields or mirrors are employed to protect the aura, and the techniques that follow can be adapted to incorporate all of these ideas. The principle behind all of these methods is intention and imagination, where the intention is used to invoke the inner senses within the imagination to create a barrier around the energy field.

Exercise - The Protection Bubble

- Sit down in a comfortable position for you (or you can do this exercise standing up).
- Close your eyes and ground yourself.
- Get a sense of your aura. Your imagination and your intuition will guide you to get a sense of your aura. You do not necessarily need to have an accurate sense of where or how it is, as a rough guide of some sort is sufficient when accompanied by your positive intention to sense the aura. Usually, your energy field extends about half a metre or so around the physical body. This will vary though, depending on how you feel on a particular day.
- When you have that sense of your aura, then imagine a "bubble" of colour that surrounds it. Gold, platinum, violet or white light are popular choices, though any colour that comes into your imagination is fine.
- Get a sense of this bubble above you, below you, back, front, left and right and all around you. In your mind's eye, get a sense of how it is. Is it strong enough? Is it complete?
- If it feels as though it needs some extra attention around you, then use your intention to breathe in and direct

positivity and strength to any areas which might need a bit of extra attention or reinforcing.

- Ensure that your bubble all around you is strong, yet flexible and is complete all around you. If there are any remaining areas that you intuitively sense require extra work, then continue to breathe positivity and strength into them until they feel complete.
- When that is completed, check your grounding and open your eyes.

As simple as this may read or sound, it is really all you need to do. However, it is important to remember that a couple of things are really essential to the process.

One is your intention. When you intend to do this in a very pro-active way from a place of confidence and belief, then it works much more easily. If you do this from a place of doubt or even scepticism, then you have a significantly lower chance of it working effectively. Another important point to remember is attitude. When you practice this technique with conviction, then again it works. When you do it "by rote" or because you think you ought to, or in a hurry without much focus, then it is likely to be less effective.

There are of course variations or adaptions to this simple technique. Instead of a bubble, like many other people you might prefer to use an egg or a pyramid, or any symbol or shape that works well within your own inner world. Some people have a preference for having a metallic colour on the outside of the energy protection barrier, as the metallic resonance of the gold (or silver etc.) reflects any inappropriate or imbalanced energy back to the Universe. It is really a question of personal preference and choice. Nobody can ever tell you that you are doing this wrong.

However, if the technique that you are using is not working for you, then try another technique. The important thing remains to make your intention clear, to have confidence in yourself and in the technique, and to develop a sense of knowing and trust that you are protected. And do remember to avoid focusing on what you are protecting yourself from as then your energy focus is on the negative, rather than on the positive energy you wish to maintain.

I recommend that you use energy protection around your energy field when you get up in the morning and before you go to bed at night. Like the grounding exercises in the previous chapter, this is something that can be practiced, learnt and then carried out quite easily and quickly. The energy protection and the grounding exercise are also combined in the exercise in Chapter 7.

Exercise - Protecting the Chakras

Another simple way to protect your energy field is by working with the chakras. If you are familiar with the chakras, then carry on. If you are unfamiliar with the chakras, then do look them up on the internet or have a quick look at the chakra diagram and brief descriptions in Appendix A of this book so that you can get a quick understanding.

A very simple explanation for the chakras is that they are energetic centres that are located in the energy body that connect with plexus (or nerve) centres on the physical body. Each of the chakras corresponds or connects with one or more glands in the endocrine system of the human body. Therefore, what happens to your chakras will affect your physical self and more importantly, your immune system via your nervous system. If some form of an imbalance is "experienced" in the chakra, then it will flow through the chakra into the nervous system and can then eventually materialise in some manner in the physical body.

As we all have an ability to perceive or take in energy, through our chakras, it is necessary to have some form of a filter system in place to ensure we are not taking in energy we do not need into our energy body, and thereafter our nervous system and physical body. The barrier method of using a bubble, or protective layer, around the aura, does an excellent job on the whole.

Sometimes though, it is also extremely beneficial to do specific exercises for the chakras. The chakras open and contract on a regular basis in line with your moods, biorhythms and your activities. For example, when you do any kind of spiritual work or experience strong positive emotions, your chakras are likely to open up, much like a flower opens. That is wonderful as it allows you to be open to positive energy.

However, you do not want to be open all of the time, and there are some situations where it is definitely preferable to have your chakras much less open. The underground system in London is a prime example of this or any other form of public transport during rush hour is equally applicable. Often, it is full of denser emotional energy, and people rarely seem to smile or radiate happiness, and you do not want to be taking in this kind of energy.

For situations such as this, it is extremely useful to have a way of opening and contracting your chakras quickly and easily. There are a few ways that this can be done. Some people talk about closing down their chakras completely, though I would advise against that. A chakra is something that is alive with vibrational energy and needs to be open, even if it is just a small amount. Therefore, what I recommend is that you use your intention to contract and protect the chakras the appropriate amount. You do not need to start thinking about this appropriate amount and what it might be; your intention is the key and will do the work for you without the need for analysis.

Exercise - Contracting & Protecting the Chakras

- Sit down comfortably (you can also do this standing up or lying down).
- Ground yourself.
- Use your intention to "contract and protect" your chakras the appropriate amount for you. As mentioned, I suggest that you avoid getting into specifics about the right amount; the intention will be enough.
- When you work with the chakras, imagine them either contracting or opening at both the front and back of your body in the corresponding areas, except for the crown which is on the top of the head and opens upwards, and the root which opens downwards.
- When doing this, start off at the crown chakra on the top of your head and then work down through your body, i.e. then continue with the third eye, throat, heart, solar plexus, sacral and root chakras. (check the diagram in Appendix A if you need to)
- Focus all of your attention on the crown area on the top of your head, and get a sense of that area contracting the right amount for you. For example, if you imagine a flower that is able to contract to a bud so that it is still able to take in a little bit of light, then imagine a similar thing happening with the chakra.

- Come down to the third eye chakra in the centre of your forehead between your eyes, and get a sense of that too. As you do, imagine that chakra area contracting the right amount too.
- Then the throat chakra - that area can gently contract as well.
- Keep on moving down through the chakras in turn. The heart, the solar plexus and then the sacral (which is three fingers below your navel) all of which have a correspondence at the back as well as the front.
- Then move down to the root, or base chakra. I advocate leaving this area open, though with energy protection all the way around it down into the earth. With the root chakra open, it is easier to stay grounded and to channel healthy grounding energy into it.
- Then move back up the chakra system and open up each chakra in turn. Start off with the root or base, then move through the sacral, then solar plexus, heart, throat, third eye and then the crown on the top of your head.
- Now practice contracting and protecting your chakras once more, moving from the crown to the root chakra.
- When you have done this, check your grounding and your energy protection are in place all around you.
- And that is it.

Note: when you are consciously opening up, perhaps to meditate or do some form of energy work, then start with the root chakra and work up through the chakras.

It is useful to practice this exercise a few times a day, and especially so if you are unfamiliar with the concept of opening and contracting the chakras. The point of practicing it is so that you can do it easily when you need to. For example, if you happen to be commuting every day, then you really do not want to be open to all of the dense emotional energy that might be present. Instead, you want to be in your nice little bubble with your chakras gently contracted. Being able to contract your energy field in this way enables you to maintain the integrity of your own energy system without getting caught up in anybody else's energy.

I recommend paying particular attention and intention at the solar plexus, as this is one of the most sensitive areas where you connect with other people and places, and often without realising it. The solar plexus is the feeling centre, and those who have heightened kinaesthetic (feeling) sensitivity in that area may often get a strong feeling or sense when they notice tension or heightened emotion in a person or place. That is an excellent reason for being more aware of this centre, and taking extra care there.

Whatever visualisation or imagination you choose to use in that area is worth doing with extra emphasis. You may even like to imagine a door in that chakra which is locked, or a band of golden energy around that area. The intention of these ideas is to fortify the chakra and prevent any unwanted, intrusive connections taking place in that area.

You may come across ideas where people suggest leaving the heart chakra, the crown chakra or the root chakra open at all times. The open heart is good for connecting unconditionally to others, the crown for opening up to the Universe and the open root chakra is good for grounding. This is a moot and very discussable point. Ultimately, it is, of course, a question of personal preference, however, it is beneficial to exercise prudence rather than throw caution to the wind.

It is far better to learn in which situations, or with which people, it is energetically healthful to have these chakras open rather than being an open house at all times. Learning to open and contract your chakras is a great way to manage and to bring balance to your energy system, and understanding where and when you need to carry this out, can enhance your life immeasurably.

Personally, I avoid contracting the root chakra, and instead I leave it open, yet protected, in order to maintain a healthful grounding energy. When I am working with clients, I keep the heart and crown open and protected, and with loved ones, I do the same. When intending protection for these areas, I imagine positive, strong energy around the chakras in question. I stress this is a matter of opinion, and perhaps confidence in one's own energy management, so see what feels right for you in this respect.

Some additional ideas for you to consider when working with the chakras in this way

- Some people imagine or visualise colours around their chakras. The colours of the rainbow correspond to the seven chakras, starting with red at the root and up to violet at the crown. When you are moving through the chakras, it can be helpful to imagine the colours expanding or contracting.
- Some people sense the chakras as flowers which open and contract from a flower to a bud. This is very useful piece of imagery for working with the chakras
- Some sense the chakras as doors, which open and close and can be locked.

Whatever adaption or variation of the technique that you use is fine, so long as you believe in its efficiency.

The next technique that I want to mention is complete confidence. Having complete confidence, or even a knowing in your ability to carry out this technique and the infallibility of your energy system does work for many people. However, I recommend that you avoid being delusional or lazy about this. The people who I have found that this method works for are generally those who are very well grounded, have been practicing the barrier methods of energy protection for some time, and regulate the opening and contracting of their chakras quite easily according to circumstances — i.e., they have already put in the practice and managed to refine it to a fine art which works for them.

It is useful to have a positive intention around energy protection work, and even some accompanying words (or perhaps a mantra), to emphasise to yourself what it is that you do. My own protection affirmation or mantra to myself is:

"I am able to maintain the integrity of my own energy field at all times and in all places, spaces, and situations."

I believe wholeheartedly in that affirmation, and I have invested a lot of energy in believing in it over the past fifteen years, and so it works really well for me and my energy system.

There are many benefits to energy protection. Life can be challenging at times, and most people have enough of their own challenges and learnings to work through without taking on the energies of other people or places as well. Inappropriate energies can affect your mood, as well as your physical, emotional, and even your mental health. You may even pick up what are referred to as energy attachments if you are unprotected, in which case you will need to clear or get them cleared as soon as possible. By the way, this is reasonably common, and it is not a reason for panic or fear. By working with energy protection techniques though, you are able to maintain the integrity of your own energy, and you pick up much less energy from other people, places or situations. This is going to leave you feeling healthier and happier on a more regular basis.

One final thought about this is that energy protection techniques can appear to be a little vague if you are finding out about them for the first time. Again, it is something you can theorise about easily enough. However, the reality is putting it into practice and then noticing the difference. I have worked with countless people over the years who have become aware of the positive benefits of energy protection techniques simply after using them for a while. When you try them out, you may well notice a feeling in your body that for some can be very tangible as a feeling of security, or perhaps relaxation. What this is really all about is being conscious of your own boundaries, and when you are conscious of your own healthy boundaries around you, then it basically allows you greater freedom to be you, and to embody your own energy, and to feel good about that.

There are other ways to work with energy protection too. Some people work with their spirit guides or angels to assist them. For those who already have an understanding in this area, this is another option for many people do this, and it can work well. Bear in mind, though, that if you are asking spirit guides, or angels to do this work for you and are fairly blasé about it, then you are not really taking full responsibility for your own energy management, and may find yourself coming undone. How I suggest approaching this is to ask them to work with you. Then, this is a co-operative venture that you are still taking responsibility for rather than simply expecting to have it done for you. If this is an area you are already working with, then you may well get an intuitive sense of how you can work in this respect. Popular choices to work with are your own guide, Archangel Michael (probably the most popular), Sekhmet the Egyptian Goddess or something from within your own culture or belief system that you resonate with.

For those who are healthily sceptical about this type of idea, then please remember that this concept is very popular in the Far East, Latin America, and parts of Africa. The idea of a God or Goddess, or Spiritual Being, protecting your home as an example is often symbolised by a statue outside, or just inside, the door of the home. Working with that "energy" to protect the self is also common. That might not solve your healthy sceptism though, and the only way to really do that is to put it into practice and see if it makes a difference for you.

For those trained in Reiki then the Reiki Symbols can be very useful— the Power symbol in Reiki II is particularly useful for this. For people who resonate with crystal energy then black tourmaline, smoky quartz, amethyst, amber, labradorite and chiastolite can all work well. Keeping the crystal in your pocket works well, as does keeping it somewhere within your energy field. Placing a protection crystal at the foot of your bed or under your pillow at night can be very useful at night. Remember, though, that the crystal does not do the work for you, so you need to work with it in a co-operative way, and also remember to cleanse it regularly.

Some people might use symbols or talismans. The cross is an obvious one, and some people wear Egyptian ankhs, Rudraksha beads from the Vedic belief system, or a special Tibetan protection symbol similar to the dorje, etc. The list is actually almost endless as there are many different things in many different cultures that work well.

Finally, a certainty or knowing that the symbol or whatever tool that you use will work for you is important. Ensuring that you are still taking responsibility for your own energy protection and not simply relying on an external resource is also vital.

> ### Soul Suggestion
> *Being conscious of your boundaries allows you greater freedom to embody your own Soul energy.*

CHAPTER 6

Clearing Your Energy

"Energy work is priceless. It makes every day extraordinary and transforms the mundane to the holy"

Silvia Hartmann

Grounding and energy protection combine rather splendidly together to ensure the integrity of your own energy system is balanced. This is especially evident when you have been practicing it for a while and are confident in the methods and the success of it. However, they are not fool proof. Everybody has their "off days" or weaker moments when they are tired or perhaps when their emotions get on top of them. And everyone is prone to have negative thoughts, feelings, and emotions and these may well hang around in your own energy system, clogging up your natural flow to a lesser or greater degree.

Therefore, as well as the grounding and protecting, it is also an excellent idea to clear your energy on a regular basis. Much as you look after your personal hygiene each day and shower or bathe to keep your skin clean and fresh, then it is prudent to do the same energetically. Using the metaphor of a house to represent you, then as well as having your house built on firm foundations (grounding), having locks on the doors and windows and maybe an alarm system (energy protection), then hopefully you also like to clean your house on a regular basis.

The frequency is down to the individual. I know some people who like to do it once a week. Personally, I like to do it at least every morning and night. That is my own personal preference for what helps me to feel comfortable, especially when I am working with a lot of clients. It is important that you choose your own rhythm and method for doing this clearing work for yourself. As ever, it is preferable to keep it reasonably simple and also meaningful so that it does not become a chore. All energy clearing techniques should be straight-forward and the couple of suggestions that follow certainly are. They are by no means the only ones, as there are plenty of ways to clear your energy field.

Whilst doing this work, you need to be mindful and keep your attention focused on your intention. I also strongly recommend that you are clear with your intention regarding where you are releasing any energy when you clear it. Send it into the Universe or down into the Earth and not out of the window where it will simply move on to someone or someplace else.

Exercise 1 — Chakra Clearing

- Ground yourself
- Protect your energy
- Imagine and intend that a shower of healing energy (you can perceive this as white light for example) flows down through each of your chakras in turn, much like being under the physical shower.
- Intend and allow for it to flow down from above the crown chakra on the top of your head down all the way to your root chakra and intend that the energy clears, balances and energises each chakra in turn, and in doing so it clears and removes any inappropriate energies, sending them into the Universe and/or to the Earth.
- Imagine the healing energy moving through the crown chakra- clearing, balancing and energising that chakra.
- Move down to the third eye chakra - clearing, balancing and energising that chakra.
- Then to the throat chakra - clearing, balancing and energising that chakra.
- Then the heart chakra - clearing, balancing and energising that chakra.
- Then the solar plexus, sacral and root chakras - clearing, balancing and energising each one of those chakras in turn.

- Intend that the healing energy shower can flow up through you as well as down and allow that to happen.
- Imagine the healing energy flowing up and down through your chakras three times. You might take a few minutes to move through each chakra, or you might do the entire process in a few minutes; either way is fine. The important thing is to do the exercise with focus.
- Then do the same with your energy body around you, again intending that healing energy clears, balances and energises the energy field around you, returning any inappropriate energies into the Universe and/or the Earth.
- When you have finished, check your energy protection.
- Check your grounding.

You can do this in a few minutes, or you can take as long as you like, perhaps even making it into a full-blown meditation for 30 minutes or so. You might also want to try my mp3 "Self-Healing Spring Clean" which is about 25 minutes in length.

You can also do this exercise in the physical shower, taking just a few minutes to use the physical energy of the water to assist your imagination and the clearing process.

Exercise 2 — the Golden Net

This is a simple variation of exercise 1 that you can also do for you in a matter of moments or minutes. It involves visualising/imagining a net (like a fishing net) which is finely woven and made of Golden Light, and moving it through your energy field.

- Ground yourself
- Protect your energy

- Intend to bring the net down through you, through your chakras, through your physical body and your energy body and your entire being to clear and remove all inappropriate energies taking them into the Universe and/or the Earth.
- Repeat this a few times.
- Check your protection and grounding when you have finished.

Note: With any energy clearing technique, if you happen to be aware of energy leaving you during the process, you do not necessarily need to know what it was, or is. You may get an awareness of a person, place, situation or one of your own thoughts. Avoid going into a place of analysis, or more especially judgement, and just let it go without dwelling on it. There is a possibility that if you are very curious and try to find out what it was, then you may draw it back to you. Remember intention and attention can result in attraction.

Additional Note: Spirit attachments might be an issue for some people. However, these are both a separate topic and a separate book. If you think you have a spirit attachment that is persistent and you cannot clear it yourself, then I suggest that you either attend a class or find a trained practitioner in your local area and book a session to get it cleared.

There are many other ways of clearing your energy. For those people trained in Reiki, the Reiki Symbols, and particularly the Power symbol in Reiki II is useful for this, as are the Reiki Master symbols.

Sound is also an excellent clearing tool. Chimes, gongs, crystal bowls and tingshas are probably the best that I have come across.

Smell is also very beneficial to clear the energy of both you and a room, and in particular frankincense and white sage work well, as well as many other types of incense.

All sorts of crystals can be useful for clearing energy too. Some enhance and maintain the energy in a room like amethyst, and others are particularly good at clearing energy with people or rooms, like selenite or smoky quartz. Something that you are drawn to is normally the right maxim with crystals, as there are many potentially suitable possibilities. On a similar note, one remarkably good way of clearing your energy field is with a salt bath which I recommend doing once a week or fortnight. Himalayan pink salt is especially good for salt bathes.

What underpins all of these ideas is intention, and whatever you use or do, always have a focused intention to clear your energy field.

An important point to consider is that cleanliness of both yourself and your space works wonders to keep your energy clear. Sound and smell are particularly excellent for clearing rooms, though sometimes the key to clearing the energy of a space is to do the physical first, and you can read about an aspect of that in Chapter 19.

Soul Suggestion
Having your energy clear is like having a clean house.

CHAPTER 7

Putting It All Together

*"Energy healing is like defragmenting your hard drive.
The scattered pieces of yourself become whole again."*

J.R. Payette

If you are reflecting on the previous three chapters of grounding, protecting and clearing your energy, then hopefully that is a positive reflection that this all makes good sense and is something that you can either put into practice or use to improve your existing practice. However, if you are thinking something along the lines of "How on Earth am I going to have time to do that in my already busy day?" then hold that thought for a minute and read on.

For a while it may seem that there is a lot of information to take in, and especially so if this is new to you, what it all comes down to is a simple practice that you could do in under five minutes when you do it mindfully and with a positive intention. Hopefully, you have time to do that for yourself?

The exercise that follows effectively puts together the summarised contents of the previous three chapters and can be done quite quickly once you have mastered it. The more often you do it, the easier it will be to do effectively and reasonably quickly, and with great results:

Exercise - Putting It All Together

- Sit down, lie or stand in a comfortable position for you
- Close your eyes
- Take a couple of breaths in and out.
- Command all parts of your energy to come back here to you now
- Ground by focusing your attention on the base chakra area of your spine and imagine it extending all the way down into the magnetic core of the Earth. At the same, intend and imagine growing roots from the soles of your feet down into the Earth centre.
- Protect — place a bubble both around you and around the space where you are — intend that you are "safe, comfortable and protected within this space."
- Imagine, intend and allow the energy of the Earth to flow up from your roots and into your root chakra and then into your chakra system as well as your feet, legs, and body and feel that connection to the Earth permanent and stable.

- Imagine and intend that a shower of healing energy flows down through your chakras, and through your energies bodies — clearing, balancing and energising each of the chakras in turn, and all parts of you and in the process releasing any inappropriate energy into the Universe or the Earth below you.
- Intend and allow this healing energy to move up through you too.
- In total do this three times up and down.
- When completed — give thanks for any help received.
- Re-affirm your protection
- Re-affirm your grounding
- Open your eyes

When you are doing any of the techniques in the last few chapters on a daily basis, remember that it is easy to allow them to become ritualised behaviours that you are doing without feeling, so try to avoid these techniques becoming a chore for you. Instead, do them with positive enthusiasm and intention. It is beneficial for your energetic well-being, so keep that in heart when you think about doing these exercises.

This combined exercise might start off being a five or ten-minute process while you are mastering it. After practice and time, you can get it down to a few minutes if you want to. It can be done quickly, efficiently and with a positive intention in the morning whilst you are showering, or at a quiet moment before you leave your home. Alternatively, you could take your time, indulge in the process and really focus on each chakra, whilst connecting with the energy and really enjoying it. Remember for yourself that a strong positive, vibrant intention is always the most important aspect. Doing it in a half-hearted manner ("oh, I really must….") is considerably less helpful for you.

I have been working with these simple techniques for years, and they have worked brilliantly well for me. I have also taught them to numerous clients all of whom have benefitted. Some of these clients have been suffering from, or have been on the verge of illness, often undergoing extreme emotional issues, and there have even been a couple of people who have been diagnosed with mental health issues. In each case, when the individual has been able to apply themselves to do the techniques with love and care, there have been notable improvements in their overall well-being, and in a few cases little miracles that have taken place.

A good point to hold in your thoughts is that these are preventative techniques that help you to take care of you in a proactive way. Furthermore, they are energy techniques, and as energy is the underlying reality for all of your thoughts, emotions, behaviours, and physicality, then these techniques may well be helping you in any number of ways in your external reality.

If you found that there has been a lot of text to read for these last few chapters, or that you take in this kind of information more easily when listening to it, then you may want to purchase my "Energy Management" CD through my website which contains all of the info and exercises for Grounding, Protection, and Energy Clearing from the last few chapters. When you purchase it, please use the discount code "ireadthebook" to obtain 50% discount off the marked price.

> ### Soul Suggestion
> *Simple, regular practice brings*
> *great strength and positive changes for you!*

CHAPTER 8

Cutting Cords

*"Love yourself enough... to cut yourself
loose from the drama-filled past...
enough to forgive yourself... enough to move on."*

Steve Maraboli

Cords are energetic ties which can connect you with other
people, life situations, objects, places, animals, or even concepts -
like a business or a project. For a visual representation of a cord,
think of the umbilical cord that connects a baby to its mother,
and then think of this as being energetic instead of physical.
Energy cords are ever present in your life, and most cords form
quite naturally in your life when you meet and bond with other

people, places, etc. and equally they usually attach and detach in a healthy way.

Loving partners, for example, will have positive cords in place between them, and these stay in place for the duration of the relationship. A baby is corded to both of its parents, and especially the mother when it is born. In an ideal scenario, these cords naturally detach over time as the child becomes more independent and less dependent on the parents.

There are these positive, healthy cords such as the mother/child bond and then less healthy cords too. The latter are ones that stay in place for longer than is appropriate for one or both parties, perhaps when a relationship is over, or when you move house, leave a job, etc. These ongoing cords can serve to maintain behaviours, situations or some other kind of ongoing attachment which usually becomes unhealthy for one or more individuals, and effectively stop you from moving on in some way.

Unhealthy cords might also be projected at you by other people; perhaps those who are jealous of your business, or maybe a person who has taken a liking to you and would like to date you or be intimate with you. There are many possible explanations for why people might energetically cord, or attach to you. The essence of an unhealthy cord, though, is that there is usually an agenda with it, and that agenda is not in line with your highest good. What that invariably means is that someone is trying to control you, or an aspect of your life and that, of course, is unhealthy for you.

If you are living a perfect, healthy life and everything in it is flowing and flourishing without any problems then perhaps cords are something that you need not concern yourself with at this moment in time. However, if you feel you are being held back, or feel limited in some inexplicable from way from something you would like to do, like thrive in a new relationship, succeed in your new job, find a new place to live, fulfil your potential in any other way, or simply that your life is not working in quite the way you imagine it could, then cutting cords is a potential area to look at in more detail.

How would you know? Perhaps there is a physical situation where you feel trapped in a relationship or a job, you have ongoing intrusive thoughts or dream about a particular person or situation, your energy levels are seriously depleted, or perhaps you are even suffering from a disease, pain or illness that does not make sense. Or maybe you get an intuitive feeling that there this is something wrong, in which case I suggest you trust that inner-tuition.

I had an Italian male client a few years ago, who had reached the age of forty without being able to move out of his mother's home. Culturally the Italian mother/son bond is often strong anyway, and this individual also had definite secondary gains to stay at home during his twenties and early thirties, namely the home cooking and getting waited on by his mother.

However, for the previous few years, he had been actively looking to move out of his mother's home and rent his own apartment. Each time he had tried to do that, something had gone wrong at the last minute to prevent him leaving. After some soul-searching, a friend advised him to look at the energetic aspects of what was going on, and that was how he came to a cord-cutting healing session.

In the session, we discovered a large cord connecting into the back of his solar plexus chakra from his mother. He felt this cord was controlling his free movement (and it was). After some considerable work, he cut the cord to his mother, whilst maintaining a different positive and loving cord in place at the heart chakra. Within a few days he started looking again for a new place to rent; within a week he had found somewhere, and within three weeks he had moved out and on.

Cords can attach to chakras, parts of body or organs, and sometimes when they attach to the latter, it can even manifest in serious illness. More often though, you will notice a cord if an area of your life is not flowing as it should, or if you feel drained of energy on an ongoing basis. If you do notice, or believe, that someone else has been cording to you in some way, then that is sort of okay. Let me explain that further by saying it is not necessarily an aggressive act on their part, as it often comes from the unconscious or simple thoughtlessness, so I would not recommend confronting them about. Furthermore, it is completely unprovable.

The exercise that follows will help you to cut cords.

Cord Cutting Exercise Guidance

Please avoid using this exercise, or the findings from it, as an excuse to project any form of negative energy at another person. The focus here is to clear the cord, heal the part of yourself that allowed that energy to become attached to you, and to move on. The other person's journey is exactly that, and if you get involved in projecting any form of negativity at them, then it is likely that you will exacerbate or prolong the situation that you are trying to clear up.

It is important to know that cord cutting does not necessarily mean you are cutting people out of your life; it does, however, mean you are cutting the unhealthy aspect of the behaviour out of your life. So, it is acceptable to work on a cord from a parent for example, as it does not mean the parent will disappear. The relationship between you and the parent, though, should hopefully change for the better after the cord cutting work.

Often after cord cutting work, the phone will ring, or a text will be received from the person who you have just cut cords to. It is uncanny how often this has happened when I work with clients on a one-to-one basis. If it is someone you are cutting out of your life as the relationship is over, then let both them and the call leave with love. If it is someone who is staying in your life, then it is your opportunity to let go of that old behaviour and instead behave in a different, more empowered manner to that someone. In this way, your interactions change and become positive and healthy.

As one final note for this exercise, I will use the word person or someone to describe who you are cutting cords to. If you are cutting cords to a job, place, object, pet or something more abstract then simply substitute your own word for person each time you read it.

Cutting Cords Exercise

Note: You can either do this exercise with someone or something specific in mind, or you can see what happens when you do the exercise, by making the intention to find any cords that might be holding you back in some way:

- Do this in your sacred space and imagine you are in a safe place
- Use your intention to cut a cord that no longer serves you
- Close your eyes
- Ground and protect your energy

- Gently open up your chakras
- Use your intention and your imagination to scan from the top of your body downwards looking for <u>one</u> negative or unwanted cord. If there are more, work with one at a time.
- You may sense a tension, or other kind of sensation or an inner knowing when you find something.
- When you do, then get a sense of the cord – its colour, shape, texture, and where it is connected to you physically and/or energetically.
- Try and get an idea or a sense of who is on the other end of the cord — you may already know – or perhaps a person or name may pop into your head.
- Get a sense of where are they corded to you, i.e., to a body part or specific chakra
- Imagine putting that person in a protective bubble and tell them that this process is for healing and positive outcomes only.
- Focus on the cord again, and get a sense of what direction the energy of the cord is flowing in? From you to them, or them to you, or both ways?
- Then, have a sense of how long the cord has been there and what the purpose is. Why they are cording to you, or you to them. Are you doing something to allow this cord? Take your time with this and allow your inner tuition to guide you in a non-judgmental way.
- What is it that you need to say to them that you have not been able to say so far? Get it off of your chest and out of your throat, and in this safe space, imagine saying those words to them now.
- Do they have anything to say to you? If so, then listen to them.

- Ensure that you both hear each other, and that you have honestly expressed everything that you needed to in order to give you closure.
- What is needed now to fully resolve this issue? Is it understanding, acceptance, an apology or even forgiveness?
- Remember that you do not have to like what happened in the past in order to understand, forgive or accept. This process is about acceptance, and that and perhaps additional forgiveness can set you free.
- Now intend to cut the cord between you. You can use anything you like, perhaps something that resonates with your imagination, for example, a sword, a pair of crystal scissors or anything similarly effective.
- Focus on your end of the cord first and using your intention ensure that all of the cord is cut and removed from you, and all residues of that cord are fully removed. The intention to do this is enough, though you may get images or sensations at the same time too.
- Then intend to fill the area where you have removed the cord from with positive healing energy - perhaps white light - and allow the energy to flow into that area to completely cleanse it. As it cleanses that area completely, you are also letting go of the old patterns, any agendas from the past and all of the energy from that cord. Continue to allow the healing energy to flow into the area where the cord once was to cleanse it completely. Let go of everything that you no longer need as that happens.
- Once it is cleansed, imagine that area filling with a protective healing energy – perhaps golden light - which can heal, seal, fully protect and nurture that area.
- Now turn your attention to the other person, and cut or remove the same cord from them. Remember that you are

doing them no harm. When the cord is cut, once again clear and cleanse that area on them with positive healing energy. Then fill the area with protective healing energy to heal, seal, nurture and protect.

- Once that is complete, ensure that you destroy the cord. Imagining burning it is the best option. Whatever you do, make sure that it is fully destroyed. So, avoid burying it in the earth or anything else that might promote future growth.
- Check how you feel now.
- Get a sense of how the other person seems now.
- Imagine filling up the other person's protective bubble with whatever positive energy you like, perhaps understanding or gratitude for the learning, or peace. Ensure that the energy you send is positive and unconditional.
- Now start to move them away from you in their bubble. And get a sense of them drifting off into the Universe until you cannot see them anymore. Remember you are sending away the unhealthy aspects of that interaction and setting yourself free in the process.
- Check you are fully surrounded by a protective bubble of light and imagine healing energy all around you healing, nurturing and protecting you as it surrounds you.
- Then ground your energy by sending roots down into the earth and take a few moments to feel grounded, protected and fully in your body.
- Rest and reflect for a while and make any notes you need to.
- Drink plenty of water over the next few hours.

Please remember the guidance given before the start of this exercise. Your phone may ring, or you may get a text from the person who you cut cords to. If this happens, then this is your chance to behave in a different way. You can, of course, use this process for all sorts of different issues and situations in your life.

> ### __Soul Suggestion__
> *Release the control that other people,*
> *places and situations have on your*
> *energy - cut cords and free yourself!!*

CHAPTER 9

Relaxing With the Breath

"Breathe.
Let go.
And remind yourself that this very moment is the only
one you know you have for sure."

Oprah Winfrey

It is becoming widely recognised that stress is the source of many illnesses and dis-eases, and in our frantic modern world there are a lot of opportunities to become stressed. Doing the opposite of being stressed is key, and it is now widely accepted that one of the obvious opposites, relaxation, is one of the most important elements for your health and well-being. Along with your general well-being, it is also vital for your inspiration and creativity. Well-known examples of that are Isaac Newton who "discovered" gravity relaxing under an apple tree; Einstein who is said to have formalized his theory of relativity relaxing in a hammock, and apparently Edison's key to perfecting the light bulb was a healthy dose of relaxation.

Many people go on holiday or wait until the weekends to relax. However, the reality is that it is optimal for your well-being that you relax whenever you can, rather than wait to do it. A simple way to do that at any given moment is by relaxing with the breath. I remember listening to a radio interview with a Doctor who had made an important medical breakthrough years ago, and he was asked by the interviewer if this breakthrough was his gift to humanity. He said that he guessed it probably would turn out to be, however, if he had been able to give a gift of his own choice to humanity, then it would be to teach everybody how to breathe correctly. His view was that most people on the planet do not breathe correctly and that undermines their health.

So, what is the deal with breathing? All of you reading this book are presumably doing so, and hopefully will continue to do so for a while...at least until the end of the book! Yes, many people do not breathe properly in the course of everyday life, and especially so when they are stressed. When people get stressed in any way, then they tend to start breathing rapidly, and their breathing will usually go only as far as the upper part of the chest;

a very shallow breath. Few people will breathe all the way into the belly, which is where they really need to be breathing into all of the time, and again, especially so when stressed.

Correct breathing activates the parasympathetic nervous system (PNS) quicker than anything else; the PNS then helps promote relaxation within a person, and increased levels of relaxation mean less stress and less illness. What happens is that the breath brings oxygen plus other vital nutrients into your body. These are then distributed through your blood to all parts of your body, nourishing the muscles, the five trillion or so cells of your body and the PNS. The shallower the breath, the less oxygen comes into your system, the less your PNS is fed, and the tenser and more stressed you are likely to be. The deeper the breath and the opposite is going to happen.

The breath is actually also the only bodily system that can be consciously and subconsciously controlled. This means that by breathing more consciously, then you can start to re-programme the autonomic systems which regulate the breath subconsciously, and what that means in simple, practical terms is that you can move from stressed to relaxed states by using the breath. Hypnosis can do the same thing. Using the breath is usually a much quicker route in, though.

As most people are programmed to breathe without really thinking about it, then some re-programming is required. A simple intention to breathe more consciously for a few minutes and a few times each day is likely to be an excellent start to re-programming yourself. When you energise and oxygenate your body fully, then both the physical body and the mind have a chance to let go and release tension. Additionally, the body and mind tend to become more in harmony with each other, which in turn helps promote harmony in every bodily system. When I teach my hypnosis courses, one of the first hypnosis scripts that the participants practice is a relaxation script where the breathing slows right down as the client focuses on it. This simple relaxation script is a very powerful process, and like many simple things in life, it is very powerful and highly beneficial, just like the simplicity of the breath.

The first step for you to practice is to develop some everyday breath awareness and observe your breathing as often as you can every day. Each time you do that, then you can focus on breathing in and out through your nose, start to slow your breathing down and then begin to breathe consciously into your belly. When you start to do this consciously on an ongoing basis over a few days or a week, then you start to re-train your breathing and deeper breathing down into the belly will start to become more automatic for you. When that happens, all of the breathes you take will oxygenate and energise you more, and help to keep you relaxed more of the time. And it is as simple as that!

It is often easier to have that outlined within the context of an exercise, so the first of the two exercises that follow is a belly breathing exercise.

Exercise 1 - Focused Belly Breathing

- Be in a comfortable seated or standing position.
- With eyes open or closed (the latter is more effective), start to focus on your breath as it comes into the body and as it goes out of the body.
- Notice how the breath is, as it comes into the body and as it goes out of the body. Notice the effect that it has on the

body, and the way it helps the chest to rise and fall, allows the rib cage to expand and contract, and the stomach to push out and come back in.

- Have a positive intention for your breath to relax your mind and your body.
- As you inhale through the nose, use your intention to breathe in relaxation.
- As you exhale through the nose, use your intention to breathe out any stress or tension.
- As you breathe in, try and breathe as far down into the body as you can. Use your imagination to allow the positive energy of the relaxing breath to flow into the belly. Avoid straining or trying too hard, and let the breathing be as natural as it can be.
- Do this 15-20 times, three times each day, for three weeks.

It should take a mere minute or two each time you do it (that is five minutes a day), and you should feel the benefits within a few days. What is more, your body will start to remember this method of breathing and do it automatically after a few weeks of practice. And you can do it anywhere you like, and whenever you have a couple of minutes spare.

Alternate Nostril Breathing (Nadi Shodhana)

Nadi shodhana, or alternate nostril breathing, has long been a feature of both Ayurveda and yoga. Rather than being limited to Far Eastern tradition, it is being increasingly recognized across the world for it has genuine beneficial health benefits. The practice is exactly as it sounds, i.e., breathing through each of your nostrils alternately. Why this is particularly interesting and effective is that your left and right nostrils have different nerve endings that connect to different parts of your brain. Breathing in through your left nostril will access the right "feeling" hemisphere of your brain, and breathing in through your right nostril will access the left "thinking" hemisphere of your brain. Consciously alternating your breath between each nostril will help to harmonise the two hemispheres of your brain.

The more specific benefits are:

1. It activates the parasympathetic nervous system and reduces blood pressure.
2. It enhances respiratory strength and endurance.
3. It improves attention and fine-motor coordination/performance.

Thus, it is effectively helpful for your hearts, lungs, and heads, and thus your entire system.

Exercise 2 – Alternate Nostril Breathing

- Be in a comfortable seated or standing position.
- Have your eyes open or closed (the latter is more effective).
- Use your thumb on your right nostril, and your little finger (pinky) and ring finger (the finger right next to your little finger) combined together for the left nostril.
- Hold your right nostril closed with your thumb and breathe in through your left nostril.
- Pause, and while your lungs are full of air, switch your fingers so that your left nostril is closed by the little finger (pinky) and ring finger.
- Then exhale out your right nostril.
- Then inhale up your right nostril, pause, and again while your lungs are full of air, switch your fingers so that your right nostril is closed by your thumb.

- Exhale through your left nostril
  Carrying on alternating between the nostrils and repeat this process about 12 times.

If you feel light-headed at the end of the exercise, then make sure you are grounded, and drink some water.

As with any technique, when you can practice it on a regular basis (rather than once in a while) then it strengthens the process for the subconscious and consequently increases the benefits for you. Once in the morning and once in the evening for a week can give you a good idea of how it works for you, and if it is something that you want to continue with. See how you feel, and if the benefits are obvious (and they should be) and then continue for as long as feels right for you. Breath is the energy of life, so whatever you do, you become more conscious of it. When you bring consciousness to any aspect of your life, it can revitalise you and your entire life.

> **Soul Suggestion**
> *The breath is life and mindful breathing can re-energise your entire day...week...month...year...life*

CHAPTER 10

Meditation

*"I have so much to accomplish today that I must meditate
for two hours instead of one"*

MK Gandhi

Meditation is proven to be highly beneficial for your health. There are reputed to be over 3,000 scientific studies on the benefits of meditation; the known benefits cover mental, physical, and emotional well-being. Mentally it can improve focus and concentration, memory retention, creative thinking, information processing, decision making, and problem-solving. Emotionally it can enhance self-esteem and self-acceptance, help to reduce worry and anxiety, help to improve your moods, enhance emotional intelligence, and lessen fear and loneliness. Physically, it improves your immune system and energy levels, breathing and heart rates, reduces blood pressure, and can work to reduce inflammation disorders and much more. It also strengthens your connection with your Soul.

People sometimes think that meditation is either complicated or that you need to attain a Zen-like state when you do it. Neither is necessarily true. One of the simplest forms of meditation is to follow the breath coming into your body and going out of it. That can be all you need to do, and now you know how to do that with either one of the exercises from the previous chapter about the breath.

Many people worry about turning their mind off when meditating, or perhaps more relevantly their inability to keep their mind focused. One popular meditation technique, Transcendental Meditation or TM, encourages the mind to jump wherever it needs to and be aware of whatever thoughts that come into the mind. By use of a mantra, which is "given" to the student in the TM training course, the user is able to slowly quieten down their mind chatter and focus the mind more and more. You do not necessarily need to take a course and get a mantra to achieve this. Instead, be aware of your mind if and when it jumps, (and it quite probably will, as that is what minds tend to do), then observe it without judgement and bring it back to the focus of your breathing.

The mind naturally offers us all a few challenges when we try and meditate. Here are a few simple suggestions for you to work with those challenges:

- Avoid giving up and give yourself time to PRACTICE.
- Avoid chastising yourself, if your mind drifts and thoughts distract you.

- Do not expect anything to happen — just enjoy the experience.

Meditation can be very inexpensive to learn if you go to a class, and there are most definitely benefits in joining a class rather than sitting at home on your own. In a class, everybody is at the same stage of learning, and others may experience the same challenges and have the same questions as you, which you can then share and reflect on. I first started learning to meditate at a Buddhist Vihara in West London where I was living at the time, and at an organization called Inner Space in Central London. Both offered free meditations classes, and there was no obligation to get involved in the belief system of the particular organisation. Both were invaluable in the development of my meditation practice which I still use today. There are hundreds, probably thousands of forms of meditations on offer, especially if you look online. The trick is to find one that you like. This is one of the most effective ones that I work with:

Million Smile Meditation Exercise

This meditation is one I adapted from a Reiki technique. I call it the million smile meditation as there have been occasions in the past when the calmness that it has helped me to instill in me have been worth a million smiles!!

It involves placing your palms together in front of your heart chakra in the centre of your chest. Whilst this is commonly known as the prayer position in the Western world, in many Eastern traditions, it is known as a gesture of respect, humility, and reverence. The connection of the two palms is used to focus the mind and express the total unity of being. It also represents the bringing together of the polarities within you (masculine/ feminine, light/dark, etc.) and the two hemispheres of the brain. The meditation itself is a connection between body, mind, and Soul and helps to promote calmness.

- Start off by sitting in a comfortable position, either on a chair or the floor, with your back as straight as you can easily manage.
- Set an alarm clock or timer for 10 minutes (longer if you prefer)
- Make it your intention to do this meditation to help promote calmness within you, and close your eyes.
- Inhale through your nose and exhale through your mouth for the duration of this meditation.
- Bring your hands together in the prayer position with your palms and fingers facing each other, and hold them together in front of your heart chakra in the middle of your chest.
- Start by observing your breathing and allow your breath to flow comfortably and easily into your belly.
- Allow yourself to get used to the rhythm of this different breathing pattern (in through the nose and out through the mouth), so it starts to become automatic for you.
- Each time you inhale, place your tongue on the roof of your mouth just behind your front teeth.
- And when you exhale, let your tongue drop to the bottom of your mouth.
- Note that breathing in this way stimulates major energy circuits in your body.
- Allow this different pattern of your breathing to continue until it starts to become more automatic.

- Then focus all of your attention on the point where both middle fingers touch each other.
- Still breathing in the same way, try to forget anything else other than the point where your middle fingers touch each other.
- When your attention wanders, and it will, then bring it back to the point where your middle fingers touch each other.
- When thoughts come up, avoid trying either to fight them or hold on to them. Simply allow them to pass by like clouds moving across the sky, as you bring your attention back to the point where both middle fingers touch.
- Avoid trying to create a specific experience based on any expectations or preconceptions that you might have.
- Simply be as fully present as you can to the place where your middle fingers touch.
- When your alarm clock or timer signals the end of the meditation, then ground and protect your energy field.

Note: 10 minutes might go by really quickly for you, and if that is the case, and you enjoyed the meditation, set your alarm clock for longer the next time you do the meditation.

I suggest doing this meditation once a day for 20 minutes for a duration of 21 days if you really want to experience its full effects.

Variation

When you have mastered this technique add in a "little" extra.

Once you have focused all of your attention on the point where both middle fingers touch each other, then ask your Soul to be more present with you.

- Avoid trying to create a specific experience based on any expectations or preconceptions that you might have.
- Try to forget everything else other than the point where your middle fingers touch each other.
- When your attention wanders, bring it back to the point where your middle fingers touch each other.
- When thoughts come up, allow them to pass by like clouds moving across the sky as you bring your attention back to the place where your middle fingers touch.
- Be as fully present as you can to the place where your middle fingers touch.
- Ground and protect when you have finished.

> **Soul Suggestion**
> *Meditation is the place where you can breathe and the Soul can be.*

CHAPTER 11

Reflection and Journaling

Reflection

"We do not learn from experience... we learn from reflecting on experience.

John Dewey

Self-reflection is a valuable form of learning, and it is highly useful on the Soul journey of self-discovery. Some simple reflective questions on the day's events at the end of that day can be a highly integrating process for many people. Such questions might be:

"What went well?"

"What could have gone differently?"

"What is there to observe about how you react or respond to everyday situations?"

"What is there to observe about how you react or respond to people who have pushed your buttons and triggered your patterns?"

"Are there any patterns regarding your behavioural, emotional, or mental processes over the past few days, weeks or months?"

"Are the same situations occurring, yet with different people?"

"Are you avoiding or engaging?"

"Are you becoming more conscious of what is happening with you in the moment?"

"What there is to be grateful for?"

These and many more are the types of questions that you might benefit from asking yourself. It is important to resist the mind's temptation to judge or berate yourself when self-reflecting. Instead, observing and assessing what you need to look at is the key. Personal reflection is an opportunity to reconsider events, thoughts, and feelings from a fresh perspective. Resist any tendencies that might be present to focus on the negative, and instead allow the art of reflection to offer you simple and safe ways to think about the positive instead.

Research has suggested that unless we actively reflect on our experiences, and question what they mean, then learning does not really happen. So, the process of reflection moves us from experience to understanding. With the aid of a few simple question likes the ones mentioned above and other similar ones, then you can make cumulative steps towards doing things in your life that bit differently and making positive changes.

Reflection with a friend, colleague or peer can be very useful, so long as though the friend knows how to deliver feedback — i.e., honest, sensitive and helpful feedback. I have a good friend with whom I have what we call "Stop Right There" moments. If one of us needs to be told that what we are saying, doing, or intending might be not the best course of action, then we have given each other permission to say "Stop Right There" to the other one.

For practical everyday purposes, this entails being clear and honest with your friend, and can thus mean having to say "No" to their plan, or thoughts, in a loving, caring way. That type of friendship, when you are on a journey of self- discovery, is invaluable, for it is rare that we can be that type of friend to our self in a truly balanced and honest way.

Journaling

This goes hand in hand with "reflections," and the only real difference is that journaling is the written act, whereas reflections can be written or spoken or even thought.

Journaling, or simply writing things down consciously, is a couple of useful things though. It is an effective and easy way to reflect and let go of the stresses of the day. When it is done every day, then journaling can even offer you a mild catharsis or release through the very act of writing. It also tends to go deeper than reflecting (though good well-structured reflection can be very deep at times) because the act of writing down your thoughts can take you deeper into the subconscious or the Soul. When you do that regularly, then you make parts of self, patterns, or processes more conscious. Quite simply, your "stuff" can surface more easily when you journal and that is useful.

An example of journaling for one aspect of life that can be very helpful is a dream journal. Everyone dreams most nights, though people often forget them by the time they have got out of bed, or fairly soon thereafter. Once you start writing your dreams down, then the tendency to start remembering them more easily begins to grow, and you do remember more. Effectively this is another muscle that improves with exercise. Try it for a couple of weeks and find out for yourself. A simple way to facilitate this is to have a pen and paper by your bedside. If you are a person that says "I never remember my dreams," then please remind yourself that intention is everything, and if you want to start remembering your dreams, then reframe your intention accordingly.

Dreams can be confusing sometimes, so the simplest thing to do is to write down everything that you can remember at first, and keep your intention clearly defined to remember as much as possible. A really good tip is to give your dream a name, and preferably one that relates to the general theme of the dream as this can sometimes help to interpret patterns more easily. Furthermore, remind yourself that you are recording your subconscious, so give yourself permission to write freely without thinking too much about what you are writing. When you do this, the chances are that you will make a few "Freudian slips," or unintentional errors that reveal something more from your subconscious.

Once you have been recording your dreams for a few days or weeks, then it may well be easier to gain some understanding of the patterns you are experiencing in dream time. A simple reality to remember is that you are the best interpreter of your own dreams. It may be that you reach out to a friend or peer to give you some insight into what you have experienced, however, keep in mind and in heart your own thoughts and feelings.

Dream journals are just one example of how you can use journaling to improve your understanding and awareness of your life. Journaling in this way is essentially an excellent way of strengthening your connection with your Soul. When writing down your spiritual, energetic or everyday experiences, you encourage the Soul with your intention, that you are actually paying attention and are actively engaging with it. As you gain deeper insights into your Soul, the depth and quality of the Soul connection are likely to improve as a result.

Another excellent variation on journaling is called "doing pages" and comes from a wonderful book called "The Artist's Way" by Julia Cameron. Doing pages involves writing three pages of whatever is in your head each and every morning without stopping to think about what you are writing. You do this every morning as soon as you get up and without fail. When you engage in this process, it really helps to clear the clutter from your mind and paves the way for your creativity to flow more easily.

Whilst doing pages is a process which is aimed at creatives, it actually works well for anything in life where you lack clarity. It was an important part of my process when I was deciding where to move house a couple of years ago, as I felt the process helped to clear the way for me to find the perfect new property. It is also often part of my process when I am undertaking a physical detox, and it most definitely assists with the letting go aspect. There are many more situations that this technique could be adapted for.

> ### Soul Suggestion
> *Reflection on your experiences is the real learning. Journaling can amplify that learning.*

CHAPTER 12

Gratitude

"Gratitude is the fairest blossom which springs from the soul."
Henry Ward Beecher

Thank you, or the equivalent in your own language, are words that most of us are raised to say on a regular basis when we receive something into our lives. It is usually seen as an act of simple common courtesy and acknowledgement of receiving something.

Interestingly, behavioral and psychological research has indicated that giving thanks makes people happier and more resilient. It is also said to help to strengthen relationships, to improve health, and it tends to reduce stress.

"Why" is a good question at this point? What happens is that when you have an attitude of gratitude, it actually raises your energetic vibration or energy levels and so helps you to attract more positive experiences into your lives. This is the Universal Law of Attraction in operation. This law states: "We attract whatever we choose to give our attention to, whether wanted or unwanted."

Most of the time you attract by default, rather than by deliberate choice. Many people "just sort of get through" their day, focusing on problems that need to be solved or on things that did not feel good or seem right, and are thus being reactive, rather than proactive. More importantly, they are often actually attracting more problems, because they get caught up in the vibration of worry, stress, and bad feelings and that is what they attract into their lives.

The Law of Attraction is always at work, whether you understand it or not, and whether you believe in it or not. Like gravity, it just IS. Scientists have proved that everything in the Universe vibrates at a certain frequency, and you attract into your life precisely what you are vibrating. By developing an attitude of gratitude and being grateful for what you have in your life, you are able to shift your focus from what your life lacks to the positive abundance that is already present. Many people take a lot of things in their lives for granted, or regret or perhaps covet what it is that they have not got. Neither is energetically healthy. The latter is actually expressing a desire which effectively emphasises the lack of that something in your life. The Universe will invariably respond to that energy vibration and reinforce the lack. Ouch!

By focusing on the reality of what you have got and being grateful for it, however little that may be, then you raise your consciousness, and you can start to attract abundance of many kinds into your life. This is something that you can do at the end of every day. It can also be part of your reflective or journaling process. Before you go to sleep at night, you can quickly review your day, simply being grateful for everything that came into your life and generate more of the same in the process. In some situations, or on some days, that can be more easily said than done. Yet, there is always something that you can be grateful for, however mundane or minute it may appear to be.

For example, food is something that you can always be grateful for. Unless you are in the wonderful position of being able to grow all of your own food, then it is a given that someone else, or probably many people, have been involved in the journey of getting that food onto your plate. Moreover, Mother Nature herself has been involved in the growth, development, and taste of that food you are consuming. That is something, and some "body", to be grateful for, and to.

The reality is that you can feel gratitude for anything and everything in your life. Your friends, your family, your health, the food you are eating today, the sun, the rain, your achievements; just be grateful for everything. As you practice gratitude, it becomes increasingly easier to find things to be grateful for. Be grateful for the gift of life. When practicing gratitude, please avoid going through the motions of saying "yeah, yeah, I'm grateful."

Instead, ensure that you really feel it and connect with the energy of gratitude.

Even if you are going through a hard time, strangely it is quite helpful to be grateful for the experience. For if you decide to view this from a spiritual perspective, then you can actually give thanks for everything that comes into your life, whether it is good, bad or indifferent. There is a reason, and often a lesson, in every experience and if you are able to accept that on some level (subconscious or "karmic" Soul Journey) that you have created it, then even the supposed "bad" stuff is something to be grateful for. Consequently, you are able to embrace the learning more easily and therefore stimulate the growth within yourself as a result. Effectively, this is acceptance, and acceptance is the first step towards healing, improvement, and growth.

Furthermore, an attitude of gratitude is one important factor that starts to move you away from the victim mindset and into one of being the creator of your reality. This is something that all of us, individually and collectively, need to overcome so that both we, and the world around us, can evolve in a different direction.

Once you can really appreciate what you have already and be genuinely thankful for it, then you are much more likely to be content, to attract more of the same to yourself in the future and to help the world around you at the same time. When you embrace gratitude as part of your life, then you can also heighten your own personal energy levels as you stop wasting your energy on regrets, resentment, anger, or bitterness. Instead, you accept and trust the process that life is unfolding exactly as it is meant to.

Exercise — Gratitude Stone

A gloriously simple exercise to practice gratitude is to work with a gratitude stone. This is a small stone that you can carry with you in your pocket, purse, bag or place on your desk. It might be a stone from your garden, something else in nature that attracts you, or even a crystal. The idea is to put it in a place where you are likely to come in contact with it during your day. Each time you see or touch the stone, it is a reminder to be grateful for what you have today, and for whatever is coming to you tomorrow. This simple act trains you to be grateful more consistently, and to radiate gratitude throughout your day. As you do that, then you empower yourself to start working with the Law of Attraction in a more conscious and positive way.

When you vibrate gratitude, positive things show up in your life. Every time you see or touch your stone, you are reminded to be grateful, and soon you start to vibrate that same positive frequency, and the Law of Attraction delivers what you vibrate. The words are of course helpful to express your gratitude. In addition, you can also feel it and radiate it through yourself.

The gratitude stone exercise is an excellent way of programming yourself to generate an attitude of gratitude. You might also like to keep a Gratitude journal for yourself; many good ones are available at reasonable prices on the internet. I also have a wonderful Life Enhancing audio also called "Gratitude," which is one of the free recordings on my App. It has had a very powerful effect on quite a few people, including the following testimonial from a client:

"I just wanted to say thank you a thousand times for the Gratitude recording and for your advice around it. As you suggested, I made it part of my daily practice just before bedtime, and it's working like a gold

mine for me. I have known for ages that being grateful is cool, that it's supposed to raise my vibration and helps to manifest things in your life and all those things of things. I guess I sort of accepted that as normal, but to be honest whilst it might have been a nice thought, I never really noticed any difference in my Ife, and I guess I'd never acted on it either.

When I started listening to your Gratitude recording after buying your App, that was then I emailed you the first time and said: "what's happening with this recording, something strange is happening." I didn't really expect you to reply as I guess you get loads of odd emails from clients, but when you did and said "Good! Keep listening every day for a couple of weeks, and start being properly grateful for the strange happenings, and then listen some more if things keep happening then I did exactly that.

That was about 2 months ago, and I might not have managed to listen in every night, but I have only missed a couple of nights since then. And my life has changed hugely! I don't want to go into too much detail as you asked me for this email as a testimonial and I'm already waffling. But I have suffered with a serious skin complaint ever since I was a child, and I have always felt awkward about it. It has led to me really struggling in relationships, friendships and often feeling socially isolated. I am now nearly 40, so I have been like that for a long time. When I discovered spirituality a few years ago, it helped me to start to feel better about me, but sitting down and doing this whole gratitude thing regularly has really been a mind-blower. I've met someone real who seems to accept me as I am, I've got the best-paid job I have ever had, and that's not so easy where I live, and I have started to become part of a regular social, spiritual network who meet up in real Ife. I have always been a bit of an internet networker and generally hidden behind a screen till now. It's amazing, and I have this whole Gratitude mp3 to thank you for. As you said to me, *it's because I did the work, but I am still super thankful for this. I am recommending your App to everyone I meet!! Thanks again."*

Of course, this is a testimonial to the power of practicing Gratitude, rather than the recording, though of course, the recording is a great tool to help you to embody that gratitude. Whatever tool or technique you decide to use to help you embody Gratitude, remember that with regular use, it will change your life.

Soul Suggestion
*An attitude of gratitude
is a life changer.*

CHAPTER 13

Positive Self-Talk

Positive Self-Talk

"Words are, in my not-so-humble opinion, our most inexhaustible source of magic. Capable of both inflicting injury, and remedying it."

J.K. Rowling

Are you a glass half-empty or half-full type of person?

How you answer this question about positive thinking reflects your outlook on life, your attitude toward yourself and the very experiences you attract into your life. Furthermore, it is highly likely to affect your levels of stress and it may even affect your health.

Positive thinking is much more than just "cotton wool" optimism. It is becoming increasingly recognised in positive psychology, mindfulness and other scientifically aligned areas of health and well-being that positive thinking can have a very powerful effect on your overall physical, mental and emotional states. Some of these studies show that personality traits like optimism and pessimism can affect many areas of your health and well-being too, and that the positive thinking that typically comes with optimism is a key part of effective stress management, and this is associated with many health benefits.

The nature of life means sometimes dealing with challenging situations and uncomfortable emotions. Positive thinking does not mean that you bury your head in the sand when these happen, start whistling cheerfully, and ignore life's less pleasant situations. Positive thinking does mean, however, that you approach unpleasantness in a more positive and productive way, so the whistling cheerfully bit might actually help. What happens is that you start to focus on more positive outcomes, rather than automatically expecting negative outcomes. If that is too much of a leap, then think about more neutral outcomes, or become non-attached to the outcomes completely. For some people, their life experiences to date might make that a little more difficult to achieve than for others. Nevertheless, it is still highly possible to succeed when you are sufficiently motivated and determined.

An integral aspect of being either a glass-half-empty or half-full type of person is the self-talk that runs through your head. For some, that can be an endless torrent of unspoken thoughts that career recklessly through their heads, and of course, these automatic thoughts can be positive or negative. Some of your self-talk will come from logic and reason, other parts of it from past situations (i.e., your personal programming), perhaps from your family or friends, and other parts even from misconceptions that you create because of a lack of information or an incorrect perception of what happened at a time in your past.

If you find yourself using words like "never" and "always" within your self-talk in a negative context for yourself such as "I could never do that" or "I always mess up when I ...." then it is indicative of some past programming, which is usually unhelpful. I suggest you start becoming more conscious of those patterns and begin the process of slowly and surely changing them.

Equally, if you find yourself thinking or saying a lot of negative words or phrases like "don't", "shouldn't", "mustn't" and most especially "can't", then this is another area that you can start becoming more aware of, and slowly and surely making positive changes.

The way to start improving your self-talk is by paying closer attention to it throughout each and every day. Do this in a curious frame of mind, rather than a critical one, and make it a part of your journaling and reflection as you observe and note patterns and situations where you are less kind to yourself. With closer observation, and with the benefit of reflection or journaling, you will find yourself becoming aware of your less than kind words more quickly, and subsequently, you will be able to reframe what you say to yourself in those moments. How you can approach this, is to think of yourself as a nurturing parent to the part of you that has those patterns and moments of negative self-talk, and guide yourself to bring in the change you desire gently and easily.

If the thoughts that run through your head are mostly negative, your outlook on life is more likely pessimistic, and so life's experiences are likely to be more challenging for you. If your thoughts are mostly positive, you are likely to be an optimist and someone who practices positive thinking, and for whom life might well be a good deal sweeter. The move from the former to the latter simply requires application plus a positive intention for change. The reality is that even someone fairly optimistic will have a fair amount of negative self-talk that could be improved. When you embrace this philosophy of being able to change your self-talk, there are many health benefits of positive self-talk and positive thinking. Researchers suggest that they include:

- Increased life span
- Lower rates of depression
- Greater resistance to the common cold
- Better psychological and physical well-being
- Reduced risk of death from cardiovascular disease
- Better coping skills during hardships and times of stress

It is unclear exactly why people who engage in positive self-talk and positive thinking experience these health benefits, however, they do, and that is the most relevant point. One theory is that having a positive outlook enables you to cope better with stressful situations, which reduces the harmful health effects of stress on your body. It is also thought that positive and optimistic people tend to live healthier lifestyles, which may be because they indulge in more physical activity and follow a healthier diet and lifestyle, and so they reap the benefits accordingly.

When you are able to take greater control of your self-talk, then you are able to focus more easily on the positive aspects of experiences, do more positive things and your life can improve in numerous ways.

An additional way to change your self-talk is through the use of affirmations, and you can read about those in the next chapter.

Soul Suggestion
What you say to your self are the most important words that you hear! Make sure they are your best words!

CHAPTER 14

Affirmations

"My favorite affirmation when I feel stuck or out of sorts is:
Whatever I need is already here, and it is all for my highest good."

Wayne Dyer

As you have read this far through the book, then you will have doubtless worked out that a large part of the underlying ethos of this book is that: "Your thoughts create your reality; whether that is good, bad or indifferent."

When you consistently observe yourself and reflect on your processes and patterns, then you are capable of improving your simpler thought patterns. Sometimes, there are thought patterns that seem a lot harder to change, and these are the ones that are more deeply lodged within your subconscious mind. These might originate from earlier in your life, from the influence of other people or they might have even come from past lives. The reality is that it does not really matter where they come from, so long as you can change them for the better, and consequently improve your everyday reality.

One way to change more deeply ingrained thought patterns is through the use of affirmations. Affirmations are statements that are used to positively affect both the conscious and the subconscious mind. When you repeat affirmations on an ongoing basis, then you can help yourself to bring change to your life, and so positively influence your behaviors, habits, actions, and reactions.

Everyone says casual affirmations to themselves throughout the day as part of their self-talk, and some of these can be ones that you say to yourself with emotional conviction. For example, you might get up in the morning and say "What a great day. I feel fabulous", or you might get up in the morning and say "Oh no, it's too early. I didn't get enough sleep. I feel awful, and I am so tired". Both statements have emotional content, and both are likely to have some bearing on how your day works out, for they help to sustain and nurture the state of mind that you are in, and thus how your consciousness creates your reality.

As you will have noted from the last chapter, the way to re-create your reality is to be more mindful of the words that are coming out of your mouth and buzzing around your mind. You can do this by becoming more aware of your self-talk, changing it and then accompanying that self-talk with positive emotions wherever possible. Furthermore, you can utilise affirmations to enhance and alter your state of mind, and to change some of those deeper patterns.

When used consciously, an affirmation is a carefully crafted statement that is repeated to yourself frequently. It can also be written down or listened to via an audio recording in order to help its acceptance into the subconscious mind. Reinforcement (i.e., repetition) is one of the main keys for success from affirmations.

Creating Affirmations

For affirmations to be effective, they need to be mindfully created, and a few simple guidelines need to be kept in mind:

1.   Keep them in the Present Tense

Phrase affirmations as if the intention of your affirmation is happening now, i.e. your goal has already been achieved.

| For example: | Wrong | "I want to be confident". |
| | Right | "I am confident". |

Start your affirmations with phrases like "I am...," "I choose" or "I have... ". Then you are telling your consciousness that "this" is happening now. Words like "I want" or "I need" are indicative of lack, rather than the having or achieving of whatever you are looking to create. I recommend that you remember this, as it is a very important point.

2.   Phrase Them Clearly & Positively

Make the suggestion completely unambiguous and always focus on the positive.

For example: Wrong   "I don't want to be shy."

Right   "I am confident and self-assured"

The subconscious mind is likely to focus on the word "shy" in the first example and amplify the energy of that, rather than the actual desire which is the opposite. Additionally, it is a commonly-held view that the subconscious mind does not hear words like "no" and "not" and instead it absorbs words and information very literally, like the mind of a child. If you say to a child "Do not go into that room...." then the next thing that happens is … the child goes into the room!

So, phrase your affirmations cleverly and carefully, and please ensure you avoid words of negation wherever possible, and make your affirmations as positive as possible.

3.   Create Them In Your Own Language

By this, I mean create them in the style of language that you use on a regular basis. I once saw an affirmation that said:

"I am overflowing with felicitations for myself on a daily basis, and it is my assumption that priceless gifts of health, happiness, and abundance are mine to behold now and forever."

This is beautiful in both the words and the sentiments that it expresses. Yes, it is very different to the style of language that I use for myself. So, I doubt whether it would be easily accepted within my subconscious mind, as I would have some conscious resistance to it. Plus, it is much less easy to remember. Simpler and easier to remember affirmations are usually far more effective:

"I love myself deeply and daily, and always say kind words to myself"

What to Use Affirmations For

Affirmations are easily adaptable to any situation in life, and you can use affirmations to assist you with a variety of purposes. Here are some simple examples:

- Relaxation — "I let go of stress, and I relax easily"
- Abundance — "I radiate abundance and attract it into every area of my life"
- Eating Habits — "I make healthy food choices that are ideal for my body"
- Work Success — "I love what I do, and I do what I love"
- Relationships - "I attract healthy, happy and harmonious relationships"
- Assertiveness — "I am enough"

You can use affirmations in a positive way to enhance how you would like your life to be i.e., "I am attracting positive opportunities into my life now."

And

You can also use them to counteract any negative self-talk patterns that you may discover within yourself. As you become more conscious of your self-talk, then you will automatically start to become more aware of repetitive phrases that you decide need to be changed, and you can use affirmations to help you do this.

As an example, let us say you have just started a new job that you are very excited, though also a little bit nervous, about. After a couple of weeks, the workload starts to increase, and you start to make excuses to yourself why you are not able to keep up with it. Perhaps phrases like "I don't know if I can do this," "I am not sure if I have the skills..." start to come into your vocabulary and thinking, and then more doubts pop in too. Your self-confidence levels start to dip, and slowly and surely you become more reluctant to get out of bed in the morning.

If you continue in this fashion, then life will become more difficult, and sooner or later you will be likely to fail in some way in your new job. However, this is where you could start to use some affirmations to start to reinforce your positivity:

- "I am confident of my abilities"
- "I find it easy to understand all of my new tasks and I accomplish them easily"
- "I enjoy the challenge"
- "I am good enough"

<u>Remember your thoughts create your reality and affirmations are one way to positively program that reality.</u>

How to Use Affirmations

It is best to work on one goal at a time with affirmations, and thus be fully focused with your energy and your intention. For example, working on motivation for exercise, building your confidence, and making healthy food choices at the same time is likely to scatter your energy too much for you to be successful in all three goals at the same time.

Focus on one goal, and then you enhance your chances of success. Then, you can use a number of different affirmations which are all related to that one goal at the same time.

- Choosing anywhere between three and five affirmations is usually optimum.
- Repeat each affirmation between 5-10 times.
- Repeat the affirmations out loud whenever possible.
- Make it your intention to repeat your affirmations a minimum of twice a day as a minimum — morning and evening — and throughout your day if you can.
- Say them with pleasure, rather than because you think you have to.
- Try and feel positive emotion with them as you say them.

Just after you get up in the morning and before you go to bed at night is good timing to reinforce your affirmations. When you are able to start off your day with affirmations, then it gives you an excellent focus on the day that follows. It is equally powerful when you say them just before you go to sleep, as it allows the possibility of the affirmations reverberating through your subconscious mind as you sleep.

Important Note: When you repeat your affirmations, think about your goal, see yourself as achieving it and then really feel the emotion that succeeding creates within you...perhaps joy, excitement, inspiration or gratitude? Feeling the positive emotion is a highly important factor that heightens the chances of success for the goal that you are achieving.

If you are in a situation where you cannot say your affirmations out loud, then it is okay to either do them silently or like a whisper. Either of these ways is actually still quite powerful, and when you are able to maintain your attention while doing them in one of these ways, some people find the process is even more powerful than doing them out loud.

Affirmation Tips

An excellent way to work with affirmations is to record your own affirmations on a Smartphone or voice recorder. Then you can play them back to yourself, and repeat them after you hear them. Note: it works best if you leave enough space to repeat the affirmation after each one as you record it. Other essential tips are:

1. Repetition - Continue to repeat and reinforce your affirmations throughout your day if you can, perhaps silently on your journey to work. Allow them to become part of your consciousness, so their reality manifests for you.

2. Consistency - Be consistent. However many times you choose to say your affirmations each time, stick to that number. Many people have favourite or lucky numbers, and if that is you, then use that lucky number for the number of times you say each affirmation. It will add to the positive energy that you are creating for you.

3. Persistence - When using affirmations you are creating new patterns in your subconscious mind. This does not happen overnight or even within a week. The subconscious mind needs time to integrate a new pattern, so allow yourself three or four weeks for the affirmations to take effect. We live in a culture of immediacy where we can

buy, watch, or listen to something immediately, so there is always internal pressure to make changes now. Resist it and give yourself time to make a permanent change.

4. <u>Awareness - After</u> a few days or weeks of doing your affirmations, it is likely that you will become much more aware of your thoughts and feelings. This may result in you adapting the wording of your affirmations slightly to suit your goal better. As well as helping you to hone your goal, it also means that you are taking more control of your consciousness, and this is a recipe for success in all areas of your life.

5. <u>Mirror work</u> –The late and loved Louise Hay is one of the pioneers of affirmation work, and she suggests saying affirmations in front of the mirror whilst looking into your own eyes. This can be an excellent tool for integration, yet you may notice resistance in your own eyes or face when doing this. If so, this can be a good cue for doing some deeper personal work on the resistance. If you are doing mirror work, then remember tip #3 above (persistence), and be gentle and kind with yourself whilst persisting.

6. <u>Using Hypnosis</u> - Affirmations are effective in a non-hypnotic state, however, when we use them in hypnosis they become even more "power-full". If you are very keen to use affirmations to make changes, then try using hypnosis. I have another book all about hypnosis available soon, where you can find out much more. Suffice to say though, that hypnosis is a state of simple relaxation where you are able to work with your subconscious mind more easily. Contrary to many misconceptions, it is not a state where you lose control; actually it is quite the contrary as you are able to take back control of many of your deeper subconscious patterns using hypnosis.

If you have not already done so, then you are very welcome to download the free relaxation mp3 on my website which is available when you sign up to my newsletter. Within that mp3, which guides you to a favourite place of relaxation, there are a couple of minutes of "silent space" where you can say your affirmations. Alternatively, you can find that same mp3 (and others) on my App "Hypnosis for Transformation".

7. <u>Truth</u> - Affirmations do not have to be true...yet. So avoiding getting caught up in the truth of it now; you are creating the truth of it.

8. <u>When Affirmations Do Not Work</u> – It usually means that there is a deeper core belief in the subconscious mind that is preventing them from having the effect you desire. That is reasonably common, and one reason why many people give up on affirmations, however, it is not the end of the story. You may be able to change that deeper core belief for yourself. If not, seek out a good hypnotherapist, regression therapist or theta healer who can help you change that belief.

Finally, here are some example affirmations you might like to use or amend for your own use:

<u>Sample Affirmations</u>

  - I am enough.
  - I unconditionally love and accept myself exactly as I am
  - Every day in every way I am better and better
  - I can do it.
  - I expect the best possible outcomes

- Everything is fine
- Relaxing with the breath helps my entire being
- I am open to accepting the abundance of life
- I attract healthy, happy and harmonious relationships into my life
- I communicate clearly and effectively
- I am grateful for everything and everyone in my life
- I have confidence in my own abilities
- I look forward to meeting new people
- I am conscious of my choices around food, and I am able to change them
- I am committed to making empowered eating choices
- I am good enough in all situations
- Thank you

> ### Soul Suggestion
> *I am a creative being in every moment of my life, and I choose to positively create my life.*

CHAPTER 15

Ho'Oponopono

*"Taking one hundred percent responsibility is the shortest way.
When we realize that it is only "our programmes" that do not
allow us to see things; when we stop blaming outside factors and
we decide to take responsibility, only then will heaven's doors
open up for us and we can reach a state of infinite possibilities.*

Mabel Katz

With Ho'oponopono you can have almost as much fun mastering
how to say the name as you can have profound healing using
the technique itself! Depending who you listen to, it originates
from either the Hawaiian or Polynesian islands. Wherever it
comes from, it is essentially an ancient practice of reconciliation
and forgiveness, and its power to help us today is the most
relevant point.

One of the principles behind Ho'oponopono is that "we are all one" and this has idea had much resonance in ancient times in locations where people lived as an integral part of the community. There was a great deal of interdependence within the family or community, and if one person behaved badly in some way, then the whole family or community would take responsibility for whatever that person's actions had been. The idea of Ho'oponopono (sometimes called a Ho'oponopono Prayer) was that it was used and communicated by the whole family or community as a means of healing whatever action, or inaction, the person responsible had taken. The idea and the potency at the core of it is the responsibility and the fact that responsibility is taken, rather than blame being projected outwards at other people.

For me, the Ho'oponopono resonates on a Soul level, as I believe that at a Soul level and prior to incarnation in this life, we have all chosen or planned for certain things to happen in our current life, whether they be good, bad, or indifferent. When we do Ho'oponopono, then this prayer connects with the Soul energy acknowledging and accepting that whatever has happened in our life is there for a reason, and thus we are taking responsibility for it at a much deeper level.

Ho'oponopono can used for a variety of "things" that happen in your life, whether they are physical, psychological or emotional, as these are all energetic at their core. I would advise against expecting a cure (especially from a physical ailment), however, do be prepared for a shift in energy which can result in positive changes happening on the physical level. I have personally used Ho'oponopono for relationships, work issues, problems with a landlord, and have seen clients work with a large variety of situations with it.

I have been using the technique on and off since 2007 when I read about it in a book by an American author called Joe Vitale who told the absolutely fascinating story of Dr. Ihaleakala Hew Len. You can easily find this story on the internet, and it is well worth reading as you will be able to get a greater glimpse of the potential power of this technique when you read it.

There are a couple of different versions of Hoʻoponopono that I have come across and used, and there are a couple of different ways of addressing the prayer too.

Version 1
I am sorry
Please forgive me
I love you
Thank you

Version 2
This is my responsibility
I am sorry
Forgive me
There is only Love
Thank you

Obviously they are quite similar, however, there is an added emphasis on the "responsibility" in the second version. Personal preference is the key here for whichever of these or any other version you use, as there is no right or wrong with a technique of this nature. Some people address the Hoʻoponopono to Spirit (God, the Universe or whatever belief system you resonate with) and some address it to the Soul. I have also heard of some people addressing it to the person they have wronged in some way. All are fine. For your information, my own personal preference is the second version and to address it to the Soul.

In reality, the words are the window dressing for what is going underneath which is the energy work, the emotional awareness, the taking of responsibility and the intention and integrity behind it all. The power of this technique is that you are moving from perhaps a place of denial and blame into a place of taking responsibility. That transition happens without disempowering yourself by feeling guilty or any other emotions that are essentially self-blaming. When you can make that shift, you essentially move from victim consciousness to creator consciousness, and there is tremendous healing and liberation in doing so.

You can use Ho'oponopono for anything you want to. Whenever you have an argument with someone or something, when someone lets you down, or when your expectations are not met in some way. Instead, you can simply pause, breathe and embrace the Ho'oponopono. The length of time between the situation that happened, and doing the Ho'oponopono may be anywhere between a few moments to a few hours, days, weeks, months or even years or decades. I have worked with it as a complement to resolution for childhood events and past lives. The technique works at whatever the point in time you do it. From your own perspective, it is better to do it sooner rather later. Remember though; the goal is to do it with complete integrity and take full responsibility, rather than doing it out of a feeling of obligation.

When you use Ho'oponopono, you can do so for an isolated incident, or what I sometimes find is that working on one event leads to other similar events. During the course of writing this chapter, a situation happened where I was financially deceived by another person. It was only on a relatively minor scale, though enough for me to be upset about. As I did the Ho'oponopono work around this situation, two other situations from 11 and 18 years ago came into my awareness, and so I did the Ho'oponopono work with those two earlier events as well. The situation from 11 years involved an old friend of mine where we both lost a sum of money. I had not heard from him since that date. By the time I finished writing a few more chapters of the book, I had an email from him, and we are in contact for the first time in 11 years.

Ho'oponopono is quite magical sometimes, and I frequently use it for that reason, whether the results are obviously tangible in the external world or not. Do keep in mind though that you are not necessarily looking for external results; as what is more important is the resolution of your own internal feelings. Ho'oponopono is simple, yet amazingly profound and effective. You can try it now as easily as this:

Ho'oponopono Exercise

- Do this in your sacred space and/or imagine you are in a safe place
- Use your intention to work on an issue that you are still carrying in some way.
- Ground and protect your energy
- Focus on your breathing for a few moments
- Focus on the issue you are working with
- Get an image, feeling or sense in whatever way is most meaningful for you of the issue
- If there are other people involved, then allow yourself to think of them too.

- Allow any unresolved emotions, thoughts, etc. to surface Use your intention to start doing the Ho'oponopono to your Soul. As you do, acknowledge the possibility that in some way you have been part of the creation of this situation.
- Do the Ho'oponopono

   This is my responsibility
   I am sorry
   Forgive me
   There is only Love
   Thank you

- Repeat for as long as feels right
- Ground and protect your energy

> ### <u>Soul Suggestion</u>
> *Release the burdens of the past,*
> *take responsibility, forgive yourself*
> *and thrive in your life now!*

CHAPTER 16

The Inner Smile

"In ancient China, the Taoists taught that a constant inner smile,
a smile to oneself ensured health, happiness, and longevity.
Why?
Smiling to yourself is like basking in love:
You become your own best friend.
Living with an inner smile is to live in harmony with yourself."

Mantak Chia

Most people embrace the idea of smiling in theory, and many probably believe that they are doing it in practice. However, the realities of modern living suggest that in practice our stressful modern lifestyles tend to reduce the number of the times that we actually might be smiling during the course of an average day. This seems to be especially true in Western society where stress factors seem to loom larger than in other countries.

Studies have suggested that smiling can have a positive effect on your mood and help to reduce stress levels, and because smiling is often contagious it even make everyone around you feel better. Smiling is highly beneficial because you release endorphins when you do it. In simple terms these are chemicals that help you to feel better about yourself, so you want as many of those as you can get. Smiling can also strengthen your immune system by making your body produce white blood cells to help fight illnesses.

Sometimes it can be challenging to start or maintain a genuine smile in times of stress. Nonetheless, studies published in the US National Library of Medicine report that the ability to smile in exactly those types of situations has health benefits. When recovering from a stressful situation, study participants who were smiling had lower heart rates than those with a neutral facial expression. Another published study found that hospitalized children who were visited by entertainers who made them smile and laugh had higher white blood cell counts than those children who were not visited.

As with many things in this book and in life, it is a great idea to be pro-active rather than retro-active. Rather than waiting for something in your external reality to make you smile, start smiling from the inside. There are many simple ways to do that, like having a photo on your computer, your bathroom mirror or your bedroom door that makes you smile each you see it, and in this simple way, you then programme yourself to start smiling more.

The ancients Taoists knew the value of smiling, and they directly related it to advantages for health and well-being. They practiced a delightful technique called the Inner Smile where you smile at your inner organs. Whilst it might seem strange at first, I recommend you try it, for it is a delightful technique that works incredibly well. I learnt it during my Tai Chi studies about 12 years ago, and have been practicing it on and off ever since.

The Inner Smile Meditation

- Sit comfortably, and close your eyes
- Smile outwardly. Use a positive memory to evoke a happy feeling. You might think of someone you love or someone who makes you laugh. Maybe you can imagine a beautiful sight or a place in nature. Your positive memory could be an image of your own smiling face or a memory of a time when you felt deeply at peace. Whatever you choose, it is fine.
- Once you have a smile on your face, start to smile inwardly. Imagine a smiling face in your mind – an inner smile
- Allow your forehead to relax, and imagine that inner smile moving to the space between your eyebrows. Allow it to rest there for a few breaths.
- The picture, the feeling, the sense of that inner smile can then flow down through your face, helping to relax the cheeks, nose, mouth, and all of the facial muscles as it flows down.
- Let it flow down through your neck. You can even gently roll your head slowly and gently from side to side as you do this.
- Continue the inner smile inwardly and outwardly

- Now smile to each of the organs in turn, and as you do breathe in the energy of the organ and thank it for all it does to sustain your Life.
- Start off with the thymus gland, which is located behind the upper part of your chest, behind the sternum. Get a sense of it, and imagine your inner smile in that area.
- Perhaps you can feel it become warm as it begins to vibrate and expand, like a flower blossoming. You may even get a sense of that area smiling back at you.
- Then move to the heart. Feel the inner smile and allow a stream of relaxation to flow into your heart. By extending the inner smile into the heart, it helps to relieves stored tension and enables a new positive pathway to be created in this area.
- Feel the heart relax and expand with loving energy. Let the inner smile grow and grow in this area, perhaps filling your heart with love and gratitude as well.
- Then focus on your lungs. Bring the inner smile into the lungs and feel your lungs soften and breathe gently. Smile with every breath in and every breath out of your lungs. Feel that smile peacefully permeating your upper chest area.
- Move the inner smile down into the liver on the right side of your body, just below the rib cage. Soften it with your smile, and rejuvenate it with your inner smile.
- Move to the pancreas which is located within the left lower rib cage. Bring the inner smile there and get a sense that it is healthy and functioning well, and happy to receive your inner smile.
- Continue around to the left to the spleen. If you are unsure exactly where it is, then just smile in what you believe to be the direction of the spleen, and you will connect with it.

- As that smiling, loving energy builds in the spleen, then allow it flow into the kidneys, in your lower back just below the rib cage on either side of the spine.
- As you smile at the kidneys, smile too at the adrenal glands that sit on top of them. Smile at the adrenal glands, and tell them that it is ok to relax. Smile at the kidneys and tell them it is ok to let go of fear.
- Then move further down into the body, and into the bladder, urethra, genitals, and perineum, and inner smile in the general area where they are located.
- Imagine that inner smile flowing through all of your internal organs, and as it does that, it can spread into the muscles and into the cells of the body, and into your largest organ. The skin. The skin, and then let your whole being become one big inner smile.
- Take as long as you want to enjoy this big inner smile.
- Ground and protect your energy at the end.
- Start to feel your contact with the floor.
- Keep smiling and enjoy your day.

Take as much or as little time as you need to do each section in the exercise. If necessary, you can spend extra time on one particular body part or organ which needs extra attention.

Smile and Enjoy!

> ### Soul Suggestion
> *Look in the mirror and smile*
> *at yourself more often.*
> *Smile outside and smile inside.*

CHAPTER 17

Mantra

*"You can use mantras to help you with any issue
and to change your life for the better."*

Thomas Ashley-Farrand

Mantra is a Sanskrit word with many possible meanings: sacred utterance, tool of the mind and language of human spiritual psychology are just a few. For practical purposes, mantra is a tool for healing and helping problems in your everyday life. Mantras can be used to help you relax; they can be used to promote energy levels, improve physical healing, assist in overcoming blocks, and to help you work with many other issues.

While the history of mantra seems to start in the Vedic Sanskrit culture over 3000 years ago, there are also instances of mantras and chanting in indigenous traditions and cultures across the world. The Aboriginals in Australia, the Mbuti tribe in Central Africa, the Melanesians of New Guinea, Tibetan Buddhists and various Native American tribes are just a few of them. In the Christian tradition, the Hail Mary is said repetitively, Roman Catholic mass has daily devotional chant-like prayers, and Gregorian chants are reputed to hold a power able to calm the mind and soothe the Soul. What all of these, and other traditions that use a similar practice, have in common is that there is a belief that repetition of a sacred sound can bring change in everyday life, and that is the goal here too.

My own experience of mantra dates back over ten years and is almost exclusively based on the use of Sanskrit mantra. When I first discovered it, the rhythm of the mantra captivated me as a way of creating a peaceful state that was something more than I had previously been able to attain in normal meditation. That alone drew me into a regular use of mantra before I discovered that certain mantras could be used for specific purposes.

My first case of specific use of mantra was with the Ganesha mantra, which remains one of my favourites to this day. The elephant-headed Hindu God Ganesha is referred to as the obstacle remover, so the accompanying mantra is used for the same purposes. The idea of the mantra is that it is directed to clear the internal disharmony (energy) that is projecting outwards and creating an external problem or obstacle.

When I was first setting up a holistic practice in London, I found that I would have weeks where the flow of clients was easy, and then weeks where the client flow was considerably slower, and sometimes even completely absent. I came to see these occasions as opportunities to work with my own inner issues. However, they could take a little time to resolve, and as my client flow had stopped, and being self-employed, that was not entirely satisfactory.

So, I decided I need to adopt a proactive and pre-emptive approach rather than a curative one, whereupon the Ganesha mantra came into my life. I found that daily use of this mantra did exactly what I needed it to. It helped me to establish a more regular flow of clients, which meant that I did not continue to have the ebbs and flows I had been experiencing up until then. This worked extremely well, in spite of the fact that I often did not have conscious awareness of what the energetic blocks were.

The Ganesha mantra is Om Gum Ganapatayei Namaha which is pronounced "Om Gum Ganna-Patter-Yay Namm-Aha"

Traditionally mantras are used or chanted in blocks of 108 times daily without a break for 40 days. My mantra teacher told me that if there was a break of even one day, then the chanter would have to start the 40 day cycle afresh. If that interruption happens, and there is an obvious excuse, such as I do not have the time today, or I cannot be bothered, etc. or even a less obvious one, like forgetting, then they are all signs of subconscious resistance coming up. When that happens, the only alternative is to work with or through the resistance, and thus starting again is the only option.

I once worked with a chant on a particular issue for the better part of 9 months. I only managed to complete the full 40 days of the mantra on the 8th attempt. During each of the previous 7 times, life's circumstances had got in the way, or I genuinely "forgot" to do the chant around the 30 something day mark. This made me even more determined to complete the mantra as there was clearly a large block sitting in my subconscious that needed shifting. Eventually, I got there.

I always note the start of the mantra cycle in my diary for good measure as it is easier to keep track of it that way, and I would recommend you do the same. Having some kind of alarm, perhaps on your phone, or another device is also a good to remind you that it is time to do your mantra. There are many highly useful mantras in existence, and many of them can be found on the internet. My own personal preference is for Sanskrit mantra, and here are some of what I have found to be the most useful Sanskrit mantras:

- "Om" – for Unity and connection
- "Om Gum Ganapatayei Namaha" - for clearing blocks
- "Om Shrim Maha Lakshmiyei Swaha" — for Abundance
- "Om Eim Saraswatyai Swaha" — for Power in Spiritual and Creative Pursuits
- "Om Mani Padme Hum" — for the connection between head and heart.
- "Narasimha Ta Va Da So Hum" - for removing negativity and creating protection

YouTube is a good source for finding the rhythm of a particular mantra, and the work of the late Thomas Ashley-Farrand is perhaps the best source.

Soul Suggestion

The human body and energy field respond to sacred sound and vibration. It goes beyond the conscious mind experience, and that is the where the growth is for us all.

CHAPTER 18

Intuitive Answers

"The pendulum of the mind alternates between sense and nonsense,
Not between right & wrong."

Carl Jung

Being able to access and trust your own intuitive answers is a real boon in life, and particularly so when you are working with energy, or on a spiritual journey. One of the goals of being on that journey is to learn to trust your own intuition as much as possible without having to rely on external sources. Trusting your own intuition can be a test in itself though, as the conscious mind often gets caught up in the intuitive process, and conscious thoughts can get confused with what we believe to be intuition. Fortunately, there are many ways you can train your intuition and start to rely on it as a valued tool.

Some simple suggestions to refine your intuition are:

1. Listen — many people have monkey minds that are forever chattering, and the intuitive voice gets lost within that chattering. Slowing down and making space for yourself is important.
2. Avoid expecting your intuition to reply to you immediately. Be patient with yourself as you would with a child learning something for the first time.
3. Avoid judging yourself, or being self-critical if you are not hearing your intuition straight away.
4. When you try to learn to listen and trust your intuition, treat it like a game and explore. Play with it and have fun practicing with a friend.
5. Remember that your body is a finely honed receptive energetic instrument, so tune in and listen to it. For example gut feelings, butterflies in the stomach, a shivering down the spine are all signals that your body is processing something at a subtle energy level. Work out what these bodily indicators mean to you by acknowledging them.
6. The more you trust, the more you start sending out a positive message to the deeper parts of your consciousness that you are paying attention. Consequently, the more these parts are likely to respond to you by giving you something to pay attention to.
7. It helps to be grounded with your energy protected when you are listening to your intuition

8. Try some tools and techniques to develop your intuition. There are many.

One external tool is a pendulum. If you have not come across one before, then a pendulum is a weighted object suspended on a cord. They vary in size, shape, and material, and might be wood, metal or crystal. It does not really matter what type of pendulum you use so long as you feel comfortable with it, and also believe in the fact that it can work for you. They all work in theory.

The basic function of a pendulum is to tap into a different level of consciousness, i.e. something that you do not consciously know already. There are a few schools of thought as to whether pendulums tap into the subconscious of the individual, the Higher Self (or Soul) or the collective subconscious. Some people believe that it is a tiny unconscious twitch within the user that causes the pendulum to move, i.e. energy follows thought. Many others believe that the pendulum reacts with the subtle energy fields around the physical human body.

The most important thing is that you believe in the potential of a pendulum to give you some answers and that you set your intention to connect the pendulum with one of the possibilities in the previous paragraph. I suggest intending for the pendulum to connect with your own Higher Self (or Soul).

Pendulums can be used to give a "Yes" or "No" answer to questions. Some people also work with a "don't know" answer on their pendulum, though personally I would question the validity of a "don't know" response from the Higher Self. I suggest sticking to the two simple variations and structure your questions so that they can be answered with either the "Yes" or "No" answer.

Note: Before you start using a pendulum to ask serious questions, get comfortable working with the pendulum. Like any tool, you can train yourself in the use of it.

Pendulum Exercise

- Make sure the pendulum's energy is clear, and that you are grounded and protected.
- Hold the pendulum in your non-dominant hand in a relaxed manner.
- Then ask the pendulum "Please show me a YES"
- Take note of which way the pendulum moves for this is your "YES" signal
- The pendulum may take some time to move, so be patient.
- Let the pendulum stop moving (or ask it to do so) and then ask it "Please show me a NO"
- Take note of which way the pendulum moves for this is your "NO"
- Now you have a "YES" and "NO" on your pendulum.
- Once your pendulum is programmed for Yes or No answers, you are ready to go.

If you are working with a pendulum for the first time, then a good way to start is to get a list of about 20 or so simple questions that are a mixture of yes and no answers and that you have no emotional attachment to. For example "Is Rio de Janeiro the capital of Brazil?" and similar questions. Then you can start asking questions of your pendulum, and make a note of how many correct responses you achieve. A really good way to do this is with a friend, and then you and your friend can ask each other's pendulums questions that the other person does not the answer to. The goal of doing that is to get more comfortable with using the pendulum and for you to feel validated in the answers. Then you can trust it more.

As a general guideline once your pendulum is answering questions about 75-80 percent accurately or higher then it becomes a worthwhile and trusted tool. Then, you can move on and design more interesting questions. It should be noted that pendulums do not help you to predict the future, so generally speaking, future tense questions are harder to get accurate answers to, though nonetheless they are worth trying with once you have practiced for a while.

When you are asking the pendulum questions about yourself or someone else, then ensure that you language them clearly i.e.

- Make sure yes or no are the only possible answers to your questions
- Avoid words like "could" or "should" in the question - instead ask "is it for the highest good of..."
- Try and avoid questions you have an emotional attachment to

I recommend that you work with a pendulum to help develop your intuition, rather than seeing it or using it as a substitute for your intuition. If you reach the point where you are using a pendulum to make life decisions for you that might affect other people as well, then you need to start considering whether this really is the best way to plan your own life.

Body Pendulum

I teach this technique on one of my hypnosis courses, and it is a very reliable way of obtaining a yes or no response from the body that can also be used as a diagnostic tool to test beliefs. It can also be used as a possible self-testing method for food, supplements, etc. that are right for you. This technique works brilliantly for 99 percent of people because the body does not lie.

When I first learnt this technique several years ago, I used it when I went to the supermarket. Once there, I tested what types of food my body was genuinely ready to consume, rather than simply what my eyes liked the look of. I held the food in question next to my body, said to myself "This xxx (food) is for my highest good right now" and used the movement of my body to determine the answer. This is a wonderful way of trusting your body to tell you what it needs, and I still do this on occasions. However, there is a downside, and that is that it can take you a very long time to get around the supermarket when you do this, plus you have to be oblivious to other people giving you strange looks!!

<u>Body Pendulum Exercise</u>

Stand with your feet approximately shoulder width apart, and on a reasonably flat surface. Flat shoes are okay; heels are not recommended and without any shoes at all is preferable. It is also useful to work with another person the first time you use this technique. Then, they can stand alongside you and can watch your body moving, for sometimes the body sway movements can be quite subtle.

- Close your eyes and relax your breath for 10 or 20 seconds
- Your partner says "yes," and you repeat and feel the word internally (alternatively if by yourself, you can say it aloud).

- You should become aware of your body being pulled forward almost immediately. This is your yes response.
- Your partner says "no," and you repeat and feel the word internally (alternatively if by yourself, you can say it aloud).
- Within a few moments, you should be aware of your body moving backwards.
- Then you have a "yes" and "no" response set up.

Continue to test the response with very simple statements that you know the answer to. For example:

- My name is ... true name (for a yes)
- My name is ... false name (for a no)
- I live in ... true place
- I live in ... false place

Sometimes people do not get a reaction or are not sure what answer their body is giving them. If you feel you are not getting a true answer, then try the following:

- Drink water —you may be dehydrated.
- Take a few deep breathes, ground your energy and clear your head.
- Make sure you are using statements, and not asking questions. **
- Perform the test again.

The body should naturally move forward for a "yes" and backwards for a "no." We are drawn towards things we like, and away from things we dislike. Occasionally, you find someone whose "yes" and "no" movements are the opposite way round. So long as you get a clear and consistent form of signaling you can still work with this.

** Note: this technique seems to work best when you use statements, rather than asking questions. So, be mindful of the words (intention) you are using when you use it.

Although you can learn the basic process of the Body Pendulum Test in a few minutes, it may take some time and practice before you feel comfortable using it. The more you practice, the more instinctive it becomes, and the more situations you can use it for. Like a hand-held pendulum, a good way to start is to get a list of about 20 or so simple questions that are a mixture of yes and no answers and that you have no emotional attachment to and practice.

Note: If you are working with foodstuffs, you can hold the food against your belly with the statement "It is for my highest good to consume this xxxx" in your head. Alternatively, you could write the name of the food in question on a piece of paper and hold that to your belly instead, if the food is not available, as the name of the food will still connect you to the energy of it.

There are many other tools and techniques for developing your own ability to hear your intuitive answers. Working with the tarot, Oracle cards and the I Ching can also be fantastic aids to train your intuition. And ensuring that your energy is grounded, protected and clear is vital to hear your intuitive answers clearly.

> ### Soul Suggestion
> *You are deeply intuitive.*
> *So, use whatever tools and exercises*
> *are necessary to help you hone it.*

CHAPTER 19

Clutter Clearing

"When we clear the physical clutter from our lives, we literally make way for inspiration and 'good, orderly direction' to enter."

Julia Cameron

Everything is energy, and a key thing to remember about energy is that it is at its healthiest when it flows, and generally does not do well when it is static. Think of another form of energy such as water, and you will remember that stagnant water in a forgotten pond does not look, smell or taste that good, whereas water from a mountain spring is quite the opposite.

Stuck energy can result in your life not moving forward in the way that you would like it to, and this is evidenced in our everyday reality, and often means that you need to let go of something whether that is physical, mental or emotional, all of which are of course energetic at their core. For some the 'letting go' is an easier process than for others. Some make the journey to a practitioner to help them with the stuckness. Others choose to do it themselves, and there are many ways to do this. Many of the techniques discussed in earlier chapters in this book are wonderful ways to move yourself forward. One of the simplest ways for you to move forward when you are stuck is to clear your physical clutter around your home. Clutter is simply stuck energy in your home, and by releasing it, you stand a very good chance of releasing yourself.

When you live with clutter around you, perhaps sitting in cupboards or storage units, and rarely use it, then you may well feel unnecessarily tired and stagnant too, and perhaps even stuck in your life. Everything that you possess is connected to you by strands of energy, and when it is sitting around doing nothing with a dull, unused energy then at some level you are going to start to mirror that.

All material possessions are simply energy, so enjoy them when they come into your life, use them well, and when they have served their purpose, let them go with grace and ease. You are really only the guardian rather than the owner of those possessions. The reality is that you do not even own the body that you are reading this book in; it is simply a temporary home for your Soul. So, embrace that the fact that everything is impermanent let old things go with joy and allow the good people at the charity shops or the recycling banks to find new homes for those possessions that have finished playing their part in your life.

Clearing your clutter is hugely therapeutic. When you clear on the external, then you are clearing on the internal too. It is also extremely useful for manifesting the life you want to live. Clear some space, and then there is an open space for some new inspiration, and perhaps something wonderful to come in and fill it. Clutter clearing does not mean you have to get rid of everything of course. However, the possessions you have and keep should ideally fill you with pleasure or positive energy when you see or use them, and those that do not or that you do not use at all can be released.

Some people only clear their clutter when they move house, and this is one of the contributory factors as to why moving house can be so stressful for many people. Many decisions have to be made on what to keep and what to throw away etc., and there will be mental and emotional hooks to all of those decisions, which adds to the stress of what is a challenging task anyway.

Rather than doing it only when you have to, it is much better to clutter clear on an ongoing basis. Then you keep your energy freer and flowing better rather than staying clogged up until the next house move, the turn of the next year or the point when you start having to look for storage units for all of your stuff. On that note, the rise of big storage warehouse like the Big Yellow, and many others, in the UK is a remarkable thing. The fact that they are so very successful is partly due to people living in smaller spaces than they used to. Nevertheless, it is also testament to the fact that many people have way too much stuff that they do not use. Often when we put stuff into storage units, whether in-house or external, we do not actually need it anymore, and it really is time to let go instead.

I learnt a valuable lesson in 2002 when I sold a house and went traveling overseas. I took a lot of my possessions to the charity shop. I also put some of what I believed to be the more valuable items into a medium sized storage unit that cost me a sizable sum of money each month. Three years later, when I next settled down in this country with a place that I could call my own, one of the first things that I did was to clear my storage unit. When I did, I realized I no longer needed the vast majority of the stuff I had been keeping in storage, so I sold it all for a relevant pittance. Having paid for three years' worth of storage, I learnt an expensive lesson in the process about when to keep "stuff."

It is worthwhile pointing out that clutter clearing is often quite challenging, either to get started with, to maintain or to finish. There are many reasons why it can be difficult for some people, and here are a few of them:

Energy Levels

You are too tired or do not have enough energy to clear clutter. The excess clutter could well be the problem with the low energy levels!

Solution: start off small with a drawer and build up to bigger cupboards. Clearing the drawer will bring fresh energy.

Just in case

People like to keep things "just in case" they might come in handy.

Comment: you are not trusting that the Universe will provide for you if you do need something which is a very negative message to send out.

Solution: trust you will have everything you need at the right time.

Identity

Some of your own identity is locked up in the items you are storing. Reminders and mementos of past times are great, however, they should be positive and inspiring memories rather than those that keep your energy anchored in the past.

Solution: Be in the present moment and be aware of who you are now; not who you were in the past.

Fear

People become afraid of sorting through their stuff because it means that their emotions might come up and have to be dealt with.

Solution: Emotions need to flow rather than being repressed, which is an unhealthy coping mechanism. So deal with the fear, let go of the clutter and allow the emotions to flow. If necessary, buy a few boxes of tissues to accompany you on your clutter clearing journey.

Security

We live in a very material world where we are bombarded with messages that having lots of stuff makes us safe and is an indicator of our status in life. This is effectively mass hypnosis in its worst possible form.

<u>Solution</u>: Use hypnosis to free yourself, rather than to succumb to relentless advertising and assaults on your self-esteem. Take back control of you for you.

There is much more that could be said about clutter clearing, and what its enormous value could be for you. For those of you that are interested, I wrote a short PDF eBook a few years ago called "Clutter Clear Your Happy New Year," which offers you a little bit more information. This can be used for areas in your home that you might choose to pay a little more attention to when you start off clutter clearing. You can find it on the Free Download Section of my website here: <u>https://www.dougbuckingham.com/document-downloads</u>

Here are Some Simple Tips for Clutter Clearing:

1. If it is hard to get started, then start off small with a drawer or a small table and get the energy flowing. Do a little every day.
2. On the other hand, if you get in the flow, then go crazy and clear your home in one go! And spot the shifts that happen when you do!
3. If you live with a partner or friend, resist trying to clear their clutter for them. That could result in a big argument. Simply clear your own clutter, and see what happens with

them. Their clutter is part of you, however subconscious that might be, so do your own stuff first.

4. If you have a lot of clutter, you may need to do "several runs" as you go down through the layers of clutter (your life). Let go of what is easy on the first run, get the energy moving and as you make progress start to go deeper into your stuff.

5. Keep lots of bins around your house so that you can throw stuff away easily. I have a waste bin in every room, and they are all emptied regularly. Experts say that as much as 80% of what is stored or saved is never used again.

6. Equally, have a charity shop bag for your output. Avoid leaving it lying around for weeks or months, and instead, keep the energy moving and make regular trips to the charity shop if you have a lot of stuff to release to them.

7. Physical cleanliness helps with energetic cleanliness. Dust, hoover, and clean regularly. It helps hugely with the energy around you and who you are. I remember that people of my Grandmother's era used to sweep their houses clean each morning on a daily basis. Energetically that is wonderful, and incidentally, it is a practice that is employed in a lot of energetically-knowledgeable countries in the Far East. Hoovering has a similar effect.

8. If necessary listen to some hypnosis first to get you in the right frame of mind, Download "Relaxation" or "A New Chapter" from my website or App.

You might even decide you want the assistance of some positive affirmations whilst clearing your clutter.

"It is ok for me to let go of the old."

"I am ready to welcome the new into my life."

9. Make a list of all the unfinished things in your life that need to be competed in some way. This might include letters or phone calls that you need to make, someone you need to apologize to, or an appliance that does not work. Then set out to complete these things, for they are all draining your energy in some way.

Remember: if you are unable to do something about your clutter, it is very unlikely that anyone else will, unless you have passed from this life. It will lie there in your home, and may well prevent your life from flowing as it might.

Final note: you might feel completely comfortable with your clutter and enjoy it and may want to keep it all; nonetheless your life is stuck in some way, or possibly every way. There is ultimately no safety in the comfort zone of your clutter because there is no movement and no growth. So, remember that you always have a choice to start things moving again.

> **<u>Soul Suggestion</u>**
> *Love your things and then let*
> *someone else start loving them*
> *when you stop loving them.*

CHAPTER 20

Love Your Self

*"You have to love yourself because no amount of love from others
is sufficient to fill the yearning that your Soul requires from you."*

Dodinsky

You are now well versed in this concept…How you feel about
yourself is one of the major keys to what you attract into your life,
for the Universe reflects back to your experiences based on the

vibration you are sending out. So, if you want to have fulfilling relationships and have rewarding experiences in life, then it is important that you start off with the relationship that you have with yourself. When you do not value yourself or feel good about yourself, then you are likely to attract people or experiences into your life that do exactly that, i.e. do not value you. Yuk!

Sometimes in life, situations or people or both have drained you of your natural ability or qualities that enable you to feel good about yourself. Your sense of your true self may have got lost a long time ago, or it may have been misplaced by a recent upset. Sometimes you may love another without restraint without getting anything in return, and the more you project your love towards that other, then the less you are able to love yourself. Whatever variation of the above you resonate with or whatever your personal scenario is, they can all be damaging to your health and general well-being if you are not loving yourself.

We live in an extraordinarily judgemental and critical society where newspapers, TV shows and other media openly judge and criticise people as supposed entertainment. If you buy into that kind of entertainment, then it will indirectly and unconsciously lead you to carry out similar patterns of behaviour on yourself. Your self-talk may well be littered with criticism and blame which emits a constant signal of "I am not good enough" into your subconscious mind, and your self-esteem will suffer as a result. Instead, you need to accept yourself for who you are, change your self-talk and start to acknowledge the things you do well and those you ought to be proud of. In short, say nice things to yourself, and do nice things for yourself more often.

There are many possible explanations as to why you are sometimes unable to love or feel good about yourself as much as you could, however more important than the reasons is the desire to change that. For when you are able to start loving yourself a little or a lot more, then your life can change and sometimes in quite dramatic and highly rewarding ways. As your outer reality is a reflection of your inner world, then when you are able to love yourself, you attract more balanced and rewarding relationships into your life. It also becomes easier to manifest your desires because your sense of self-worth is improved and quite simply you feel better about yourself and attract better things into your life.

Your feelings about yourself and your everyday life may have already improved after reading this far in the book, and perhaps they will improve even more after reading through this chapter in particular. However, it is much more likely you will get even better and longer lasting results integrating some of the techniques in this book into your life. What you also need is the motivation for change, and the determination to make it happen, and most importantly of all some definite action.

As soon as you make a decision to start loving you more and more, then the inner you will respond in positive ways. Sometimes that can be a subtle change, and sometimes that can be one of those earth-shattering shifts that leaves you wondering if this is really true. It may even be that any transformation you experience takes place over some time, and it is only comments from other people that help you to realise how much you have changed. Whatever the measure of your success, know that your life will transform and improve when you start to love you!

So, how do you have a love affair with yourself? For that is exactly what you are going to be doing if you follow the guidelines and purpose of this chapter. The difference between dreams of change and actual change is invariably the actions that you take, so here are some actions that you can take which will enable you to significantly shift your thinking and feeling about you.

1.   Intention — What do you Want to Achieve?

Your intention to make positive changes for you is the most important thing. The Universal Law that says energy follows intention means that it naturally follows that the energy of your thoughts, emotions, and behaviours will start to shift as soon as you make your positive intention. So, write your positive intention for your self-love project down on a piece of paper, a journal, or even in the space below and get started with you. Your intention might be something as simple as "I intend to love myself more every day" or perhaps something more specific "I intend to love me more so I attract the perfect partner into my life."

Note: Just like affirmations, keep your intentions phrased in the present tense, i.e. as if it is happening already and without any negative words, i.e. without "no's" or "nots"

My intention is:

2.   Start learning that you are Number 1 — Put yourself first

The world "selfish" often gets a bad press as it is associated with unpleasant character traits. However, one definition of selfish is that it means looking after the self-i.e. self-care. If you are in any doubt what this might mean in practical reality, then remember the safety demonstration videos that are played on an airplane before you take off. These talk about what you need to do if an accident happens and how to use the oxygen masks in this eventuality. And what they tell you is how absolutely ESSENTIAL it is to take one for yourself before you try and put one on your children, or the person next to you.

When you put yourself first, you are able to take care of yourself first and THEN your loved ones. When you put yourself second in the airplane safety situation, you might run out of oxygen and might not be able to help anyone! And that is merely a small reflection of what can happen in real life when you constantly put yourself second. For when you set up a pattern of behaviour that puts others first on a regular basis, what becomes established in your consciousness is a pattern or thought form that effectively says "I am not as good as others," and that is seriously unhelpful for you, and moreover this is simply untrue in anybody's case.

Therefore, reflect and re-evaluate what it means to put yourself first, and more especially the areas and relationships in your life where you need to start putting yourself first at least some of the time. Work out how you can spend a little more time to start engaging in your interests, pursuing your goals and ambitions, and ensuring your well-being, for it is heartily important to have healthy boundaries in place to make sure you are getting enough you.

3.   Practice Saying the Word "NO" - to others

"NO" is a tiny little word. Sometimes, though, it can be a hard word to say, and with some of the people or situations in your life, it can be particularly challenging. If that is the case with you, then make a list of those people and situations, and reflect on how you can start to do things differently.

If there is a particular person that you need to start saying "no" to on a more regular basis, then start slowly saying "no" in nice, polite assertive ways that leave you feeling ok or good, rather than an aggressive or angry "no" that are much less helpful for you. If you are someone who is really challenged by the concept of saying "no" then you can even imagine or visualise yourself saying "no" before you actually do it in real life. If you are one of those lovely people who says "yes" to everybody and everything, and then finds out that you do not have enough time to take care of your own needs, then you need to start putting some healthy assertive boundaries in place, and quick!

Obligation can be a funny thing when it comes to saying "no." Often there are unwritten rules in place that seem to dictate that you are obliged to do certain things 'just because'. These type of situations are usually with your family, your partner, with your friends or work obligations. If you are in a relationship, and your partner is open to this type of discussion, then it can be highly worthwhile to discuss what the unwritten rules are in your relationship. A discussion of this nature can revolutionise your relationship. In any case, it is most definitely worth reflecting if any of these situations apply to you saying no. If they do, then assess whether, or most probably how, you need to start doing things differently. When you do anything out of obligation, and especially over a long-term period, it often leads to resentment. Doing things because you genuinely want to do them is a very different energy, and it is likely to have a very different effect on your immune system and your overall well-being, and that relationship.

4. Do Things That You Love - and Be Grateful When You Do

Do something that you love as often as possible, and if possible, do it each day. Big things or even really small things that take up only a little time are fine because you probably lead a busy life and time is sometimes challenging to find. Simple pleasures though, are potentially so very "powerful" for you. It could be creating a home cooked meal, perhaps making the time to spend five minutes standing still in nature, having a fun conversation with a friend or watching an episode of your favourite series on DVD.

When you do these things, take time to say "Thank You" to yourself. As you will have already read in an earlier chapter, gratitude connects you with the vibration of love, and it heightens your ability to generate that well-spring of self-love within you.

5. Reward Yourself — You Deserve It

Buy yourself gifts and reward yourself on a reasonably regular basis. This sends a message to yourself that says "I love you." Whether there is, or is not, someone else in your life to buy you gifts, or if that someone simply does not do it often enough, or at all, then please make sure you do it for you.

I need to press the pause button here and say that doing this step does not mean that you have to run up an extensive credit card bill on gifts. You can keep it really simple, perhaps by buying yourself flowers, making some fresh, healthy food, creating a home-made greetings card or yourself, doing the Inner Smile (chapter 16) or however you would like to be gifted. Treat yourself as you would like to be treated.

6. Mirror Work — Simple Genius

As you will have already read in the affirmations chapter, mirror work can be especially powerful. So, every day, or even twice a day, just before you start cleaning your teeth, you can look in the mirror and say to yourself...." I love you."

It can be as simple as that. Look into your eyes in the mirror and say to yourself "I Love you," and do this several times. Note: do make sure you are looking into your eyes when doing this, i.e. your intention is focused and mindful.

7. Recognise Your Qualities

Recognising your qualities is something that you should always have time to do on a regular basis. Sometimes, you have wonderful people in your life who tell you how "fabulous, amazing and brilliant" you are on a regular basis and that is great. However much more important than that, is when you can identify your qualities and traits for yourself, and believe them. This is not an act of self-aggrandisement or being big-headed in any way; this is about recognising your true self and connecting with your strength and inner resources in a powerful yet grounded and realistic way.

Start off by making a list of what your qualities are. There is a table at the end of this chapter where you can do that, or you can use the free e-book on my website here https://www.dougbuckingham.com/document-downloads/where some of the content of this chapter is also available.

When you do this exercise, as well as helping you to feel better about yourself, it also improves your knowledge of yourself. When you recognise and accept your very own qualities and strengths, then you start to raise your self-worth in all aspects of your life. The moment you begin to believe that you are worth it is exactly when you start to feel better and better about you.

<u>Note</u>: If for any reason you are struggling to name your qualities, then start off small. Can you smile? Can you laugh? If you write down "I can laugh" or "I can smile" to start off with, then you can build your list over a period of time as you maintain this love affair with yourself.

8.   Let Go of the Labels

In the past, many of you have been given uncomfortable and unhelpful labels, perhaps by others, or even by yourself. Maybe these are criticisms, insecurities, doubts or other labels that have somehow got attached to you, and have subsequently slowed you down in some way. These labels will be "singing a song" somewhere on the subconscious level, and that is why you have to address them. One way to work with these labels is to divide a piece of paper into two by drawing a line down the middle of it. On the left-hand side make a list of the labels you believe you are carrying. Focus on the list and write down everything that you are aware of that you call yourself, perhaps "calling yourself stupid" when you get things wrong, or perhaps your parents or siblings had a name for you when you did not get a good report at school.

Avoid attributing blame as you write these labels down, and simply make the list as short or as long as it needs to be. Then on the right-hand side of the same piece of paper, write down how you would really like to be labelled. For example, perhaps "stupid" becomes "smart enough" or "Genius." Once you have reframed all of the labels from the left-hand side with a positive label on the right, then start to cross out the left-hand side labels. Make this a conscious process as you do, and say to yourself "I am ready to let that old label go" as you work through the list. Remind yourself of the label on the right when you delete the left one.

If you get stuck, and for example say a memory of your sibling calling you this name or that name comes up as you look at a particular label, then that is okay. It may be that you need to go a little deeper into the issue, and perhaps cut cords with your sibling, or do some Ho'oponopono for the situation. Otherwise work through the list as you need to in a matter of minutes, hours, day or even weeks. You may even want to amplify the energy of some of the new labels with some affirmation work to reinforce the process.

Another way to work with these labels is by using my life Enhancing Audio "Love Your Self." As you have read this far in the book, then you are clearly determined to enhance your well-being and your life in some way, and in order to help you with that you can use the same discount code from earlier in the book which is "ireadthebook" when you buy it from the checkout at my website shop.

If you are aware of any labels that you feel you are carrying around with you that are limiting or preventing you from loving yourself enough, then you can work specifically with them when you listen to the audio. Otherwise, you can simply work with it, without concentrating on specifics and something will pop into your consciousness while you are listening to the audio. The idea of letting go of these labels is to let the real you shine through.

9.   Forgive Yourself

Let go of more of the past. "Everyone makes mistakes, and mistakes are simply golden nuggets of wisdom by which we learn" is a lovely little truism that I learnt for myself a few years ago. Miss-takes in relationships, finances, personal decisions can be reminders to think before you act, however, they also embrace much greater lessons. When you remember this, it can help you to forgive your so-called failures, and understand that they happened for a reason. When you forgive yourself, you can get closure for the past and then you can redirect your energy to new efforts that produce new results. Doing some Ho'oponopono around this is great energy medicine, and again the audio is very useful to supplement the self-forgiveness.

There are many more tips and techniques that could be mentioned here. However I wanted to keep this offering relatively brief and manageable. Hopefully, any or all of these 9 solutions will empower you to start that love affair with yourself and to celebrate you and your worthiness as often as you can.

In exercise one that follows, you can make a list of all of your achievements, both big and small. I also recommend that in addition to the exercise in this book, you make a BIG list of your achievements, and include the seemingly trivial ones too. Unless you have just popped out of your mother's womb in the last couple of years, and that is unlikely if you are reading this book, then it is certain that you have accomplished a large number of things in your life. I am not talking about walking up Mt. Everest here. Instead, I am talking about the simple everyday stuff that you do and do not give yourself credit for. Holding a heavy door open for someone, smiling at people on the tube, saying thank you and meaning it. These are all examples of you bringing positive energy into a situation that might not have been there otherwise. So, start giving credit where it is truly due, and that is with you.

Listing your accomplishments and achievements really works wonders for programming the part of you that might be resisting loving yourself, so try it now. It is very good for creating more of those achievements and accomplishments for the future too, and that does include the bigger ones as well.

As a final note, I am sure that by now you realise that self-love and self-esteem are really important to your emotional, physical, psychological and spiritual wellbeing, and thus your whole life. This chapter of the book is intended to assist you on the journey to re-establish and renew your own levels of self-love. Please be aware that it is a process and a journey rather than a moment of enlightenment and a quick fix. So take time for yourself, be patient with yourself, and continue that journey of loving yourself some more.

> **Soul Suggestion**
> *Love yourself silly!*
> *Everything else in your life*
> *will flow when you do.*

Love Your Self Exercise One: "Your Magic"

In each column write down three things that fit under those categories that you really like. Perhaps you even love those things, or they make you feel good immediately when you think about them. Do it quickly, intuitively or instinctively if you can, so without thinking too much. You can write more ideas if you do it quickly, however, avoid lingering over this exercise and write anything that resonates with you. Remind yourself of your magic!!

Achievements (Small & Bigger)	Gifts to Myself	Things I'd Like To Do For Me

Love Your Self Exercise Two: List Your Qualities

I recommend that you do this exercise three times. Ideally, a minimum of one week apart and even better if and when you have listened to the audio "Love Your Self."

My Qualities 1st Time	My Qualities 2nd Time	My Qualities 3rd Time

CHAPTER 21

Routine is the Route In

*"It's the repetition of affirmations that leads to belief.
And once that belief becomes a deep conviction, things begin to happen."*

Muhammad Ali

We all live in a culture of immediacy and instant gratification. If you really want something, and assuming you have some funds or a credit facility of some kind, then you can go online and buy it straight away, whether its food, clothes, stationery or anything else you care to name. Usually, it will arrive in the post or by some kind of delivery service within a few days. When you want information, then you turn on a computer, or look at your phone and there it is! I could continue with examples, though I am sure the point that I am making is clear by now. This immediacy is how the world is, and many aspects of that are of course very helpful.

However, every aspect of you does not function in this way. In fact, far from it, and for those conditioned to something happening now, that can present a problem when it comes to making changes on a personal level. The body learns behaviours through muscle memory over a period of time, and you learn processes through repetitive learning, and when you do either of these things you store a lot of that learnt functioning in the subconscious parts of you. Within your subconscious, there are a series of habits, behaviours, thought forms, emotional responses and more that come together to make up your own personal programming. You are a being comprised of many different programmes (whether you like that thought or not, you are) and when it comes to making a change of some kind in your life, the culture of immediacy that you live in does not necessarily have the same sway to affect change immediately within your subconscious. Unravelling an old pattern and establishing a new one often takes longer than simply pressing a different button to make a change.

For example, perhaps you decide to start thinking a fabulous new thought to replace an old dysfunctional one and to start bringing positive improvements into your life. Perhaps "I can do it" replaces "I cannot do it" for a particular circumstance in your life.

It might happen that the new thought changes your life there and then. However, it is much more likely that repeated thinking of that thought (plus "something extra") is most likely to change your life as you find yourself thinking it, feeling it and "doing it" over a period of time.

Scientists are now able to prove what most of us in the self-improvement / spiritual / energy world have known for a while. That is, a new thought establishes a new neural pathway. However, it is the repetition of that thought on an ongoing basis that makes that new neural path fully established…or almost. The "something extra" that I referred to in the previous paragraph is the emotion that comes with the idea of that new thought becoming permanent in your everyday reality. The emotion of establishing the new thought is necessary to create profound and permanent change, partly because we need to feel it to make it more real and partly because we need to use as many of our senses as possible when creating our future.

Once the thought that creates, and the emotion that it generates are in place, and other senses are thus engaged over a period of time, then effectively your energy system has changed, the new reality has been established, and different circumstances start to happen in your life. In the hypnosis and regression courses that I run, I call this future creation, for it is exactly that – how we create the future. I have already written in the introduction of this book how important it is to practice these techniques on a regular basis, and that is also what I am emphasizing here. Do these techniques in this book routinely and regularly, and your world can change in those positive ways that you desire. In this respect, routine is the route in!

You may prefer words such as "Dedication," "Self-Nurture," "Commitment" rather than "Routine" when you think about your own personal self-development, and that is fine of course. Whatever words, whatever process, whatever tools you need to work with are all fine, so long as you are prepared to sit down and regularly help yourself to do what you need to do for you.

Whatever you do, a form of "Routine is the Route In" is likely to be a necessary key to you making permanent, powerful change for you. There are many ways to do that. Hypnosis is one very powerful way to effect new patterns in your life. Most commonly, hypnosis is a combination of what happens over a series of sessions that take place plus ongoing listening to the recordings from that session that work together to help you shift you from A to B, combined with your positive intention to initiate change for you. That is why the audio recordings that are mentioned in Appendix C might be beneficial to help you with some of the techniques.

Whatever you decide to do or you, stick to it for a while and give it time, so you can allow your new routine to be the route in to your goals and dreams, and the positive life changes that can come along with that. It might be slightly contrary to the current cultural beliefs at the moment. Nonetheless, it will work for you when you persevere.

> **Soul Suggestion**
> *Your Soul understands rhythm, for the Universe is a series of rhythms and patterns. When you create rhythm in your own life, then your life expands in new directions.*

CHAPTER 22

Essential Basics

*At the beginning of every role I take, I have
to start from basics and build it up.
It's like a new construction."*

Kim Cattrall

We always need to take care of the basics, and many of the techniques offered in this book are the basics. Nevertheless, I have met several people that seem to think that being spiritual, or of an energetically-aligned temperament negates the need to take care of the physical body. Very rarely does this turn out to be the case as the body is the home for the Soul in this lifetime, and in most cases that home needs to be fairly well maintained. So, I am going to recap just a few of the essential basics that you, your body and Soul might need. Some of these are blatantly obvious, nonetheless, you might pick up a few tips by scanning through what follows:

Sleep

Make sure you are getting enough quality sleep. It is restorative in nature and essential to human well-being. Sleep deprivation is a method of torture, so avoid doing it to yourself. Ideally, remove yourself from all TVs, computers, mobile phones et al for at least an hour before bedtime. See if you notice the benefits of turning off the Wi-Fi at night, and how much better you sleep when you stop using your mobile phone as an alarm clock and remove it from your bedside. A cheap alarm clock on the internet can cut down on the "electromagnetic" pollution while you sleep, and bring your more health benefits than you might realise.

Drink water

Not everybody seems to embrace the concept of drinking water which is odd, as it is pretty much the most important thing that we could consume (barring the breath). Water is essential to life, and we need about 2 litres a day. When we do not have water, we become lethargic, tired and confused, and our skin pallor, digestion system, and internal organs are all affected.

Exercise

Exercise is not a synonym for gym! However, it is a must for most of us as our bodies need it. It helps to keep muscle tone, burn calories and keeps our metabolism active and working. Exercise may be as simple as a 30-minute walk three times a week, and anyone can easily achieve that by simply "losing" the car keys and actively planning a bit more walking into your daily routine.

Being In Nature

Research shows that environments can increase or reduce your stress levels, which in turn affects how your nervous, endocrine, and immune systems are working. An unpleasant environment can cause you to feel anxious and other negative states and emotions, whereas a pleasing environment reverses that.

Nature works and heals. It was one of the main principles of doctors sending their patients away to the seaside to convalesce during Victorian times. Being in nature, and even viewing scenes of nature can help to reduce stress and increases positive feelings. Exposure to nature contributes to your physical wellbeing, reducing blood pressure, heart rate, muscle tension, and the production of stress hormones.

Studies have demonstrated that time in nature, or scenes of nature, are associated with the experiencing of positive moods, and psychological wellbeing, meaningfulness, and vitality. And of course, it is refreshing. Research done in hospitals, offices, and schools has found that even a simple plant in a room can have a significant impact on stress and anxiety. So, work out how to work it into your life.

Spend Less Time Near a Screen

Yes, really! It is unhealthy. Studies show excess hours spent in front of TV or computer screens is directly associated with depression. Other studies show that excessive screen time is associated with loss of empathy and a lack of altruism. Read more books of the paper variety!!

> ### *Soul Suggestion*
> *The basics are what make the clock tick, the body breathe properly, and you FLOW!!*

FOOTNOTE

There is a lot of information and techniques in this book, and if you are new to this area, then you might be wondering where to begin. If you are new to all of these concepts, then hopefully that's from a position of excitement.

My brief guide for experimenting and integrating them is as follows:

<u>Chapters 1,2 & 3</u> are mainly informative and are worth keeping in mind and heart on an ongoing basis.

<u>Chapters 4, 5,6, 7 & 12</u> are essential energy medicine and I believe should be practiced daily. The same could be said of Chapter 8 for those of a more empathic nature.

<u>After that, the remaining chapters</u> except Chapter 19, 20 and 21 are ones that you may want to experiment with, practice for a short time and see how they work for you. They are all concepts, or techniques that I have used effectively in my own life, and shared with friends and clients, who have also used them equally effectively. As I hope I have stressed in the book, most of them are ongoing practices rather than one time occurrences, and potential Gifts For Your Soul.

Chapter 19 – is something you may like to look at on a regular basis

Chapter 20 is an ongoing process for the majority of the human race – do this if you do nothing else

Chapters 21 and 22 – are essential to re-emphasise the basics, and the importance of practice

And if you need any more guidance after reading this book, then do feel free to email me via my website www.dougbuckingham. com

The download section of my site is: https://www.dougbuckingham. com/document-downloads

And you can also use my site to link to the various social media outlets you can find me on.

With Love & Gratitude

Doug Buckingham
xxx

Doug Buckingham

APPENDIX A

The Main Chakras

The Main Chakras

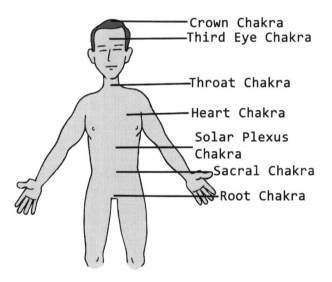

This is a brief guide to the seven main chakras (a Sanskrit word meaning "wheel") together with the corresponding glands, bodily functions, and the colours and crystals commonly associated with each chakra. The chakras have been mentioned several times already, and for those of you unfamiliar with the chakras, this may help you to understand them a little more.

The seven main chakras are energy centres that are located within the aura, and they synthesise and conduct subtle energy into the physical body. As they also energetically correspond to the glands of the endocrine system which monitors and influences all the functions of our being, the chakras are hugely influential on our everyday reality. They connect, both physically and energetically, to the major nerve plexuses of the physical body in the relevant area and so can be thought of, and even felt, as areas of greater sensitivity within our physicality.

The chakras all energetically vibrate to different frequencies of energy and colours (which is an energy vibration) and have different qualities and life learnings applicable to them. They can also be thought as information centres, in the sense that they often relate our history or biography back into our biology. For example, if a person has an issue with feeling safe then it is likely they have an imbalance in the energy of their root chakra. Equally, physical dis-eases can be traced back to the chakras; for example, many auto-immune diseases also correspond to the root chakra. There are many wonderful books which explore the chakras in much more detail, and they can be easily found on the internet. I particularly recommend Anodea Judith's books, or Caroline Myss' audios if you would like some in-depth knowledge.

This brief interpretation of the chakras is just for guidance, and is an opinion only:

First Chakra

Names:	Root or Base Chakra (Muladhara)
Location:	Base of the spine (perineum)
Colour:	Red
Element:	Earth
Functions:	Gives vitality to the physical body, Life force, survival, and grounding. "Connects to the fight or flight response."
Learnings:	Matters relating to the material world success, the physical body, mastery of the body, grounding — connection to the earth, stability, security, stillness, health, courage, patience.
Areas:	Adrenals, bones, teeth, nails lower intestines, hips
Crystals:	Red jasper, Black tourmaline, bloodstone, hematite, smoky quartz

Second Chakra

Names:	Navel or Sacral Chakra, (Swadhisthana)
Location:	The width of three fingers below the navel.
Colour:	Orange
Element:	Water
Functions:	Procreation, physical force, and vitality, sexuality, creativity.
Learnings:	Emotions, desire, pleasure, sexual/passionate love, movement, family, working harmoniously and creatively with others.
Areas:	Reproductive organs, spleen, digestive tract, kidneys
Crystals:	Carnelian, Orange calcite, citrine, topaz

Third Chakra

Names:	Solar Plexus Chakra (Manipura)
Location:	Centre of stomach - Midway above the navel & below the sternum.
Colour:	Yellow
Element:	Fire
Functions:	Vitalizes the sympathetic nervous system, digestive processes, metabolism, emotions, and centre of personal power.
Learnings:	Will, personal power, authority, energy, mastery of desire, self-control, radiance, warmth, gut instinct, trusting the self.
Areas:	Pancreas, Liver, stomach
Crystals:	Citrine, calcite, malachite

Fourth Chakra

Names:	Heart Chakra (Anahata)
Location:	Centre of the chest (to the right of the physical heart)
Colour:	Green or Rose Pink
Element:	Air
Functions:	Circulation, The link between the physical and spiritual aspects of a person The balance of giving and receiving, Self-love
Learnings:	Divine/unconditional love, forgiveness, compassion, balance, understanding, balance, oneness with life, acceptance, harmony, contentment.
Areas:	Thymus gland, physical heart, lymph system

Crystals: Aventurine, Dioptase, Emerald, Green Fluorite, Green Tourmaline, Malachite, Morganite, Peridot, Kunzite, Rhodochrosite, Rose Quartz, Tugtupite, Unakite

Fifth Chakra

Names: Throat Chakra (Visuhuddhi)
Location: Throat area
Colour: Light blue
Element: Ether
Functions: Expression of creativity.
Learnings: Being able to express from the heart clearly. Divine Will
Areas: Thyroid and parathyroid glands; neck; shoulders.
Crystals: Turquoise, Aquamarine, Sodalite, Kunzite, Aqua Aura, Blue topaz, moldavite

Sixth Chakra

Names: Brow Chakra, Third Eye (Ajna)
Location: Centre of the forehead, between the eyebrows
Colour: Indigo (dark blue)
Element: Light
Functions: Vitalizes the lower brain (cerebellum) and central nervous system, vision.
Learnings: Insight, intuition, imagination, concentration, clairvoyance, peace of mind, devotion, wisdom, perception beyond duality.

Areas:	Pituitary gland, eyes. Note: the pituitary gland which is the master gland of the endocrine system and closely related to the hypothalamus and thus homeostasis
Crystals:	Lapis Lazuli, Sodalite, Amethyst, Herkimer diamond, azurite, azeztulite, Petalite, moldavite

Seventh Chakra

Names:	Crown Chakra (Sahasrara)
Location:	Top of the head
Colour:	Violet sometimes white
Element:	Thought/intention
Functions:	Vitalizes the upper brain (cerebrum)
Learnings:	Oneness with the infinite, selfless service, unification of the Higher Self with the human personality, wisdom, continuity of consciousness, perception beyond space and time.
Areas:	Cerebrum; pineal gland. It influences the central nervous system and is also considered to be the centre for spiritual insight, vision, and intuition beyond human consciousness.
Crystals:	Amethyst, clear quartz, moldavite, purple fluorite, phenacite

APPENDIX B

Exercises in this Book

Chapter 4 - Grounding 1 - <u>Breath Awareness</u>
Chapter 4 - Grounding 2 - <u>Growing Energetic Roots</u>
Chapter 4 - Grounding 3 - <u>Grounding From the Base Chakra</u>
Chapter 4 - Grounding 4 - <u>Combining Roots & Base Chakra</u>
Chapter 5 - Protection 1 - <u>The Protection Bubble</u>
Chapter 5 - Protection 2 - <u>Contracting & Protecting the Chakras</u>
Chapter 6 - Energy Clearing 1 - <u>Chakra Clearing</u>
Chapter 6 - Energy Clearing 2 - <u>The Golden Net</u>
Chapter 7 - Grounding, Protection & Clearing - <u>Putting It All Together</u>
Chapter 8 - <u>Cord Cutting</u>
Chapter 9 - Breathing 1 - <u>Focused Belly Breathing</u>
Chapter 9 - Breathing 2 - <u>Alternate Nostril Breathing</u>
Chapter 10 –<u>Million Smile Meditation</u>
Chapter 12 - <u>Gratitude Stone</u>
Chapter 14 <u>- How to Create Affirmations</u>
Chapter 15 - <u>Ho'oponopono</u>
Chapter 16 - <u>The Inner Smile</u>
Chapter 18 - <u>Pendulum Exercise</u>
Chapter 18 - <u>Body Pendulum</u>
Chapter 19 - <u>Read the 10 Simple Clutter Clearing Tips</u>
Chapter 21 <u>- Love Your Self Exercises</u>

APPENDIX C

Available Audio Recordings

There are a series of Life Enhancing Audios available in my website shop https://www.dougbuckingham.com/product-category/life-enhancing-audio/ many of which are also available on my App "Hypnosis for Transformation." They are not essential to the processes described in this book. However, they all help to complement the exercises and suggestions in this book, and you may find one or two of them useful.

– Relaxation
– Keeping Clear Boundaries - Energy Protection
– Self-Healing Spring Clean - Energy Clearing
– Cutting Cords
– Taking Relaxing Action
– Gratitude
– My Glass Is More Than Half-Full - Improve Your Self-Talk
– Problem Solving - Intuition Building
– Letting Go With Ho'oponopono
– The Inner Smile
– Sleep Well Tonight
– Motivation to Exercise
– Being More Mindful

- Love Your Self – discount available with the code "ireadthebook"

Energy Management CD – For Grounding, Protection and Clearing Your Energy - discount available with the code "ireadthebook". This Album is also available as a DIGITAL DOWNLOAD via Bandcamp on https://dougbuckingham-solutionsforthemindbodysoul.bandcamp.com/album/energy-management

ABOUT THE AUTHOR

Doug Buckingham

"Be the Change That You Want to See in the World"

M.K. Gandhi

Doug Buckingham started off life being challenged to "make ends meet" in Essex in England. Whilst on the way home from working in London one day at the age of 21, he had a simple, yet life-changing moment, after which he changed a limiting belief about money in his own head, and almost immediately started to earn a very good income. He subsequently became a Director of a very successful International Shipbroking company, until deciding to take what turned out to be a permanent sabbatical at the age of 35.

After selling his house and car, he travelled the world extensively before coming back to the UK with the notion that he needed to get his chakras "fixed." The inner journey then followed the outer journey, and Doug immersed himself in training courses, studying as a spiritual healer for 2 years at the College of Psychic Studies, training to be a Reiki Master/Teacher, a Theta healer, an Aura Soma practitioner, an EFT practitioner and as a Hypnotherapist and Regression therapist. During that time, he also volunteered for the Fairtrade Foundation, worked for the Mental Health Charity Mind for 3 years, and created a small charity designed to help empower the people of Nhkata Bay in Malawi.

Nowadays, Doug is a trainer, therapist, and a talker about all things spiritual and energetic. He is primarily a Past Life and Regression Therapy expert and has run Hypnosis and Regression training programmes in South Africa, Mexico, Scotland, and England, as well as running workshops in Italy, Belgium, Switzerland, Lithuania and Ireland and various parts of the UK. His main website is www.dougbuckingham.com and he is the Founder of Cara — the Centre of Transformational Learning www.caracentre.com, as well as being the creator of the App "Hypnosis for Transformation" which is available at the App Store or on Google Play. He offers talks, webinars, workshops and longer courses on a regular basis.

Doug is in the very fortunate position of doing what he loves, and loving what he does. He is very privileged to get to meet and work with many amazing people during the course of his work and accompany them on part of their Soul journey through this human experience, and has worked with and trained 1000s of people.

Printed in the United States
By Bookmasters